BASIC Hydrodynamics

To Georgina

BASIC Hydrodynamics

A C Thompson, BA, PhD

Lecturer
Department of Civil and Structural Engineering
University of Sheffield, England

Butterworths
London . Boston . Durban . Singapore . Sydney . Toronto . Wellington

First published, 1987

British Library Cataloguing in Publication Data

Thompson, A. C.
BASIC hydrodynamics.
1. Fluid dynamics—Data processing
2. BASIC (Computer program language)
I. Title
532′.05′02855133 QC151.7

ISBN 0-408-01391-5

Library of Congress Cataloging in Publication Data

Thompson, A. C.
BASIC hydrodynamics.

Bibliography: p.
Includes index.
1. Hydrodynamics—Data processing. 2. BASIC (Computer program language) I. Title.
TC171.T48 1986 627′.042 86-20723

ISBN 0-408-01391-5

Phototypeset by En to En, Tunbridge Wells
Printed and bound by Page Bros. (Norwich) Ltd

Preface

This book is about using computers to solve problems involving the flow of fluids. The reader will be aware of the importance and increasing spread of computing throughout modern life. It is of course well established in science and engineering. In education, pupils will probably encounter microcomputers at an early stage. The best way of learning about computers is to use them. Using computers to solve engineering problems often helps the student to understand the subject through the logical analysis required to write a program. The programming language BASIC was designed to enable students to use computers easily and it is now the language of all microcomputers. The programs in this book are written in BASIC.

If the reader has avoided contact with computers, he or she will certainly not have avoided contact with water. Although applicable to other fluids, the theory of flow treated here is developed with applications to water flows in mind – this is even suggested by the title hydrodynamics. It is possible to live without the theory, if not without the liquid, but some understanding of the basics of fluid flow should be of use to engineers seeking to design works to convey, control or collect water. The subject should also be of interest to those concerned with structures standing in or even moving through a flow. A useful foundation for this understanding is the theory of a frictionless, incompressible flow and this is the field covered by this work. It may seem at first sight to be a restricted study but in fact it may be applied not only to flows past streamlined shapes but also to flows of water in the ground, waves on the surface of the sea and structures controlling large flows in rivers, etc.

The computer has affected the methods of hydrodynamics no less than other areas of engineering. Instead of a multitude of special solutions, each one arrived at by ingenious mathematics, we see a few more general approximate solutions using the computer to model the flow in arbitrary shapes. These methods may even allow solutions where none existed before, for example in the case of free surface flows including gravity. Even the old analytical methods can be viewed in a new light using the power of the computer to generate graphic displays of the flow. The book attempts to introduce both these perspectives by including some programs with graphic output and some simple finite difference, finite element and boundary element programs.

Each chapter after the first is designed to integrate the study of a topic with computing in BASIC. (The first chapter is a brief introduction to BASIC). A typical chapter starts with sections on essential theory where information relevant to the following examples and problems is explained. After this come the worked examples. Every example has an outline of a problem with a computer program to solve the problem and samples of the input and output from the program. A set of program notes explains the working of the program by giving the function of each group of statements in the order of their appearance. A number of problems using the programs from the worked examples or short programs to be written from the essential theory sections are included at the end of the chapter.

The chapter topics start with an introduction to BASIC computing. Chapter 2 then gives the fundamentals of potential flow theory which will be used to calculate flows which can be regarded as frictionless. Some analytical expressions for potential flows are also given. In Chapter 3, computer based methods for solving potential flows are outlined and applied to a simple potential flow. Chapter 4 applies potential flow methods to the solution of groundwater flows. Exact solutions are given for comparison with the computer methods. Finally, Chapter 5 considers free surface flows including linear waves and flows from jets, etc.

The author would like to acknowledge much valued help and encouragement from colleagues at Sheffield University and former colleagues at RMCS Shrivenham.

Thanks are due to Miss Janet Stacey for her expert preparation of the manuscript.

A. C. Thompson

Contents

Chapter 1

Introduction to BASIC

1.1 The BASIC philosophy

The computer programs in this book are all written in the language BASIC (Beginners' All-purpose Symbolic Instruction Code). This was developed at Dartmouth College, USA, as an easy-to-learn general purpose programming language. It was intended for use on time-sharing computer systems but it is now the main language associated with microcomputers and so is in widespread use. The language is not only easy to learn but also very easy to use. It is simple to type the program into the computer, run it, correct any errors, and then run it again to obtain the required output in a short time.

BASIC is sometimes criticised for leading to programs which are not structured but this is not important for short programs such as those included in this book and it is not difficult to write structured programs if required, with a small amount of forethought.

This book is not an instruction manual on BASIC. Many of these are available if the reader needs one, and some are listed in the bibliography at the end of this chapter. The book does aim to help in the learning of BASIC by applying it to a suitable engineering subject. If the reader studies the examples, copies them and runs them, perhaps with different data, and then tries some of the problems, this aim should be met.

A short description of the simple BASIC language follows to help the reader in getting started.

1.2 Elementary BASIC

1.2.1 Mathematical expressions

One of the main objects of the programs in the book is to solve the equations that arise in hydrodynamics. These contain numerical constants, variables (e.g. y) and functions (e.g. $\cos(y)$).

All numbers are treated in the same way whether they are integers (e.g. 16) or real (e.g. 16.2). An exponential form is used to represent large or small numbers (e.g. 1.62E5 represents 1.62×10^5). Numeric variables are represented by a letter or a letter followed by a digit (e.g. A or A2). On many computers π is directly available to the user either as PI or as a key. An operation such as a square root can be done by using an in-built function (e.g. SQR(X)). The argument in brackets (X) can be a number, a variable or a mathematical expression. For trigonometrical functions (SIN(X), COS(X), etc.) the argument is interpreted as being in radians. Other functions include a natural logarithm and its exponential (LOG and EXP), ABS, which selects the absolute value of the argument, and INT, which selects the integer part of the arguments.

Mathematical expressions also contain operators such as plus, minus, etc. These operators have a hierarchy in that some are performed by the computer before others. In descending order of hierarchy the operators are

to the power of (∧)
multiply (*) and divide (/)
add (+) and subtract (−)

So, for example, any multiplication in a statement is carried out before any addition. The computer works from left to right in an expression if the operators have the same hierarchy. The use of brackets allows any of these operations to be overridden. Hence

$\frac{a+b}{3c}$ becomes (A + B)/(3*C) or (A + B)/3/C.

1.2.2 Program statements

A BASIC program is a sequence of statements which the computer carries out one after the other. As it follows this program the computer allocates values to each of the variables. The values of some of these variables are determined by input of data and others are generated in the program. The assignment statement does this. It has the form

line number [LET] variable = mathematical expression

The word LET is usually optional and therefore omitted. For example, the root of a quadratic equation

$$X_1 = \frac{-b + \sqrt{b^2 - 4ac}}{2a}$$

can be found from the statement

```
100 X1 = (−B + SQR(B∧2 − 4*A*C))/(2*A)
```

It should be noted that the assignment statement is not an equation but an instruction to the computer to give the variable on the left-hand side the numeric value of the variable on the right-hand side. So we can have a statement

50 X = X + 1

which increases the value of X by 1 every time it is executed. Each variable can have only a single value at a time unless it is subscripted (see Section 1.2.7).

Every line in a BASIC program is numbered (it is possible to have more than one statement on one line) and the lines are executed in the order of the line numbers.

1.2.3 Data input

Interactive or 'conversational' programs allow the user to specify the values of variables in response to prompts from the computer as the program is running. The statement which does this has the form

line number INPUT variable 1 [, variable 2, . . .]

e.g.

20 INPUT A, B, C

When the program is run the computer prints ? as it reaches this statement and waits for the user to type values for the variables; e.g.

? 5, 10, 15

makes A = 5, B = 10, C = 15 in the example above.

An alternative form of data input is useful for large amounts of data or data which will not be changed every time the program is run. In this situation we can use a statement of the form

line number READ variable 1 [, variable 2, . . .]

e.g.

20 READ A, B, C

with an associated statement (or statements) of the form

line number DATA number 1 [, number 2, . . .]

e.g.

1 DATA 5, 10, 15

or

```
1 DATA 5
2 DATA 10
3 DATA 15
```

DATA statements can be placed anywhere in the program. It is convenient to place them together where they can be easily changed, say at the beginning or end of the program.

It is sometimes necessary to read data from their start more than once in a single program run. This is done using the statement

RESTORE

1.2.4 Output

The results of calculations and data from which they were made are output by a statement of the form

Line number PRINT list

The list can contain variables or expressions, e.g.

200 PRINT A, B, B*B/C

text enclosed in quotes, e.g.

10 PRINT "INPUT A, B, C IN MM"

or mixed text and variables, e.g.

300 PRINT "PRESSURE IS"; P; "N/MM∧2"

The items in the list are separated by commas or semicolons. Commas give tabulation in columns each about 15 spaces wide, while a semicolon suppresses this spacing. A semicolon placed at the end of a list suppresses the line feed. If the list is left empty a blank line is printed. It is good practice to use PRINT statements with READ/DATA statements so that a record of the data is obtained, and it is a necessity with INPUT statements so that the input required is indicated. In some BASICs a message can be printed as part of the INPUT statement to give a 'prompt' for the input data.

1.2.5 Conditional statements

It is often necessary to enable a program to take a certain course of action if some condition is fulfilled. This is done by a statement of the form

line number IF expression 1 conditional operator expression 2 THEN line number where the possible conditional operators are:

=	equals
<>	not equal to
<	less than
< =	less than or equal to
>	greater than
> =	greater than or equal to

For example, a program could contain the following statements if it is to stop when a zero value of A is input

```
20 INPUT A
30 IF A < > 0  THEN 50
40 STOP
50 . . .
```

In this example, note the statement

line number STOP

which stops the program running. The statement

line number END

may be used at the end of a program but is not essential.

1.2.6 Loops

It is common to have a group of statements repeated in a program and this useful feature can be achieved in a number of ways. The simplest is to use a statement

line number GOTO line number

at the end of the repeated section. This could be used with the conditional statement example above to continue the program, requesting values of A repeatedly until the user inputs the value zero.

The usual way of obtaining loops is by starting the loop with a statement of the form

line number FOR variable = expression 1 TO expression 2 [STEP expression 3]

The step is assumed to be unity if omitted. The finish of the loop is provided by the statement

line number NEXT variable

where the same variable is used in the FOR and the NEXT statements. Its value should not be changed in the lines in between.

A loop could be used, for example, to read N sets of data and print their reciprocals, e.g.

```
10 READ N
20 PRINT "NUMBER", "RECIPROCAL"
30 FOR I = 1 TO N
40 READ A
50 PRINT A,1/A
60 NEXT I
```

Loops can also be used to generate data. An example of this is the simple temperature conversion program that follows

```
10 PRINT "CENTIGRADE", "FAHRENHEIT"
20 FOR C = 0 TO 10 STEP 5
30 PRINT C, 9*C/5 + 32
40 NEXT C
```

1.2.7 Subscripted variables

It can often be very useful to give a number of different values to the same variable in a single run of a program. Take the case of a program containing data for different flow rates in a pipe, for example. It is convenient to call these Q(1), Q(2), Q(3), etc. instead of Q1, Q2, Q3, etc. A single statement can then perform calculations for all the flow rates, e.g.

```
50 FOR I = 1 TO N
60 V(I) = Q(I)/A
70 NEXT I
```

This finds the velocity of flow in a pipe of cross-sectional area A for each flow rate. When a subscripted variable is used it is necessary to allow space for all the values which will be associated with it. This is done with a dimensioning statement, of the form

line number DIM variable 1 (integer 1) [, variable 2 (integer 2), . . .]

e.g.

```
20 DIM V(20), Q(20)
```

This allows up to 20 values of V and Q. The DIM statement must be made before the first use of the subscripted variables.

Some computers allow a so-called 'dynamic' dimensioning statement, e.g.

```
20 DIM V(N), Q(N)
```

where N has been specified previously. This has the advantage of saving storage space when a small problem is solved.

1.2.8 Subroutines

Quite often a group of statements will be required at several points in a program. Instead of writing the statements at each point we can put them in a subroutine and use them with a statement

line number GOSUB line number

The program will branch to the second line when it executes this statement. This line will be the first line of the subroutine, which ends with a statement

line number RETURN

and the program then returns control to the line immediately following the GOSUB statement.

Subroutines can be placed anywhere in the program but it is better to position them at the end, separate from the main program.

If a procedure is to be used for more than one program it is sensible to write it as a subroutine. This then forms a separate unit which can be tested, proved and used unaltered in the new program. It is sometimes desirable to use less common variable names in a subroutine (e.g. X9 instead of X) so the same variable name will not be used accidentally with a different meaning in another part of the program.

1.2.9 Other statements

Remarks, headings and explanatory matter which is not to be output can be included in a program using

line number REM comment

Any such statement beginning with the word REM is ignored by the computer. These can be placed on the same line as other statements in some computers.

Non-numeric data (i.e. words) can be handled by string variables. A series of characters within quotes is called a string (e.g. "PRESSURE") and a string variable is a letter followed by a $ sign (e.g. A$). When headings need to be changed, string variables are particularly valuable and also when a question with the response Y or N is included in a program.

Multiple branching can be achieved with statements like:

line number ON expression THEN line number 1 [, line number 2 . . .]

and

line number ON expression GOSUB line number 1 [, line number 2, . . .]

When a program reaches one of these statements it will branch to line number 1 if the integer value of the expression is 1, to line number 2 if the value is 2, and so on. An error message is printed if the expression gives a value less than 1 or greater than the number of referenced line numbers.

Functions not built into the BASIC language can be defined using a DEF statement. For example

10 DEF FNA(X) = X∧3 + X∧2

defines a cubic function which can be recalled later in the program as FNA (variable) where the variable is substituted for X. The statement is clearly useful when an algebraic expression has to be evaluated several times in a program.

1.3 Checking programs

Most computers give a clear indication if there are grammatical errors in a BASIC program, by printing an 'error in syntax' message. Program statements can be modified by retyping them completely or by using special editing procedures. Most syntax errors are easy to locate but some 'mystifying' errors can occur if, for example, a variable has been used with different meanings in different parts of the program.

Not only must the program be grammatically correct, it must give the correct answers too. A program should be checked using data which give a known solution or one that can be found by hand calculation.

If the program is to be used with a wide range of data or by users other than the program writer, it is necessary to check that all parts of it function. It is also important to check that the program does not give incorrect but plausible answers when nonsensical data are input. It is quite difficult to make programs completely 'userproof' and they become much longer in the process. The programs in this book have been kept as short as reasonably possible and may not be fully 'userproof'.

1.4 Versions of BASIC and different computers

The majority of examples in this book use a simple version of BASIC that should work on most computers.

There is one important feature that distinguishes computers, particularly microcomputers with visual display units (VDUs). This is the number of columns available across each line and the number of lines that are visible on the screen. Simple modifications to some of the example programs may be required to fit the output to a particular microcomputer.

Various enhancements to BASIC have been produced since its introduction. These include the ability to use longer variable names (e.g. VELOCITY instead of V1), more powerful looping and conditional statements, and independent subroutines which makes structured programming more natural.

Structured programs can be written in ordinary BASIC using the GOSUB statement described in Section 1.2.8. A separate subroutine is written to do each identifiable task in the program and communicates only with the main part of the program, or perhaps one other subroutine. The main program then consists essentially of a list of tasks, performed by calling the subroutines, and perhaps some conditional statements. One advantage of doing this is that a library of subroutines can be built up which are useful in more than one program. The subroutines can be read in before starting to write a new program, which may then involve simply writing the main part calling the subroutines. The reader may be able to make more use of this technique than appears in the book, particularly in the graphics sections of programs, which may have to be altered for a particular computer anyway.

Graphics are probably more machine dependent than any other feature of BASIC. In this book it seemed desirable to include some sample routines for displaying streamlines and wave profiles in spite of the fact that they are written for one type of micro. The machine used was an APPLE.

Another facility which is available on only some machines is the ability to perform matrix operations by writing simple statements; for example, inverting a matrix by the statement

```
MAT A = INV(A)
```

This has been used in a few programs in Chapters 3 and 5, which were run on a VAX machine. These are lengthier calculations, resulting in a large matrix equation to be solved, and would possibly require excessive time on most micros. The larger and faster machines generally have matrix statements in their BASIC.

Very long, repetitive calculations usually need to be run as compiled BASIC rather than in the normal interpretive mode, where each line is translated from BASIC to machine code every time it is executed. The VAX BASIC does this as a matter of course, which is another reason why the time-consuming programs were run on that machine. However, many micros now have BASIC compilers and the calculation methods which now seem rather slow will undoubtedly become feasible on many more machines soon.

1.5 Bibliography

1. Alcock, D., *Illustrating BASIC*, Cambridge University Press (1977).
2. Forsyth, R., *The BASIC Idea*, Chapman and Hall (1978).
3. Gottfried, B. S., *Programming with BASIC – Schaum's Outline Series*, McGraw-Hill (1975).
4. Kemeny, J. G. and Kurtz, T. E., *Basic Programming*, Wiley (1968).
5. Monro, D. M., *Interactive computing with BASIC*, Arnold (1974).

Chapter 2

Potential flow fundamentals

ESSENTIAL THEORY

2.1 Stream function

We start by examining the flow of an ideal fluid in two dimensions. The flow will be taken as steady and the simplifying assumptions will allow it to be described by one or other of two potential flow functions, stream function or velocity potential. There are relatively simple methods for finding these potential flow functions.

The stream function can be explained by referring to some simple flows. If there is no friction, the flow between two parallel plates must be evenly distributed across the gap between them. The velocity will be equal all the way across as there is no friction to retard fluid near the walls. We may therefore say that one-quarter (say) of the total flow occurs in the first quarter of the width of the channel, as shown in Figure 2.1. If we imagine floats or streams of

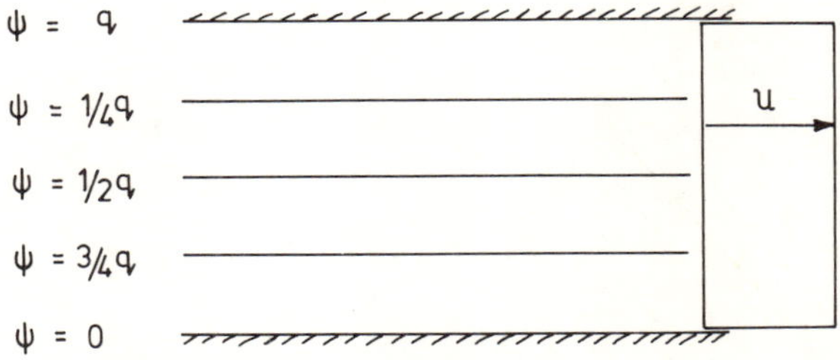

Figure 2.1 Stream function in a uniform flow

dye introduced at regular intervals across the channel they will mark out paths, and between each pair of lines there will be an equal flow. These lines are called streamlines. The flow between a streamline and a reference streamline is called the stream function ψ. This number is then constant along a streamline and distinguishes that line from any other. The velocity at any point can be found by the spacing of streamlines near the point. The flow between the lines divided by their distance apart is the velocity; i.e.

$$V = \frac{\Delta\psi}{\Delta n} \tag{2.1}$$

The direction of this velocity is of course parallel to the streamlines.

This can be seen clearly in another simple flow, that between two straight walls which converge towards a point. The streamlines in a flow with no friction must be radial lines of equal angular spacing; see Figure 2.2. Here we know that the velocity increases as the walls get closer together, and indeed the streamlines show this.

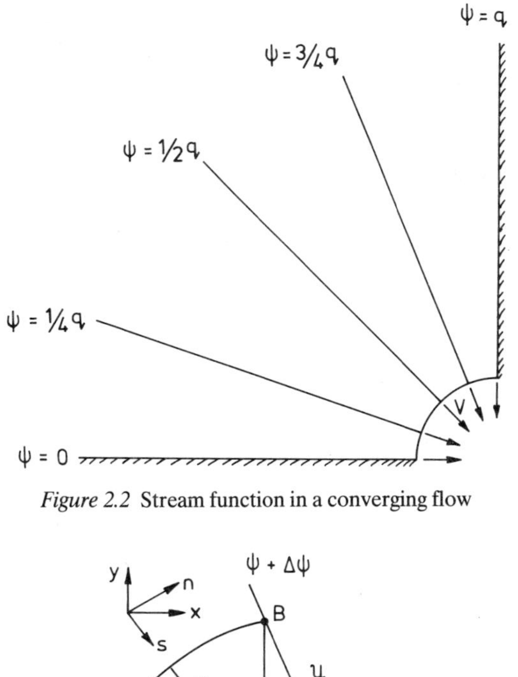

Figure 2.2 Stream function in a converging flow

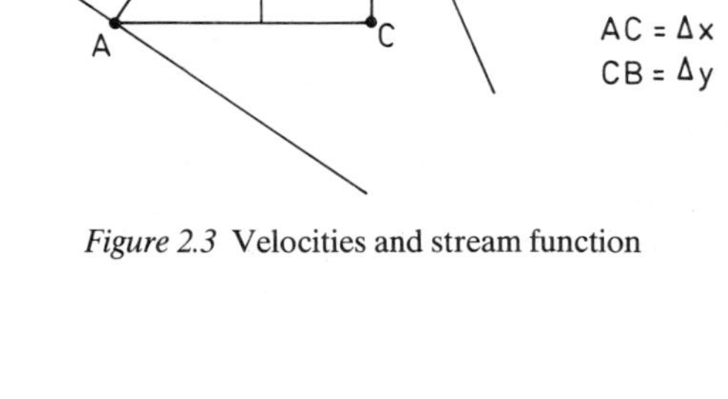

Figure 2.3 Velocities and stream function

We can also show that the velocities in the x and y directions come from ψ by considering part of this flow in Figure 2.3. By equating the flows in and out of the fluid element,

$$V\Delta n = u\Delta y - v\Delta x$$

This is the same as saying that ψ (which represents flow) increases by $\Delta\psi$ between A and B even if you calculate the change along AC and CB, so

$$\Delta\psi = \frac{\partial\psi}{\partial y}\Delta y + \frac{\partial\psi}{\partial x}\Delta x$$

hence

$$u = \frac{\partial\psi}{\partial y} \text{ and } v = -\frac{\partial\psi}{\partial x} \qquad (2.2)$$

2.2 Velocity potential

The velocity potential ϕ can now be described in a similar fashion. Suppose we relate the velocity V to a gradient of ϕ along the streamlines instead of across the streamlines, then

$$V = \frac{\partial\phi}{\partial S} \qquad (2.3)$$

or $\Delta\phi = V\Delta S$ or $\Delta S = \Delta\phi/V$.

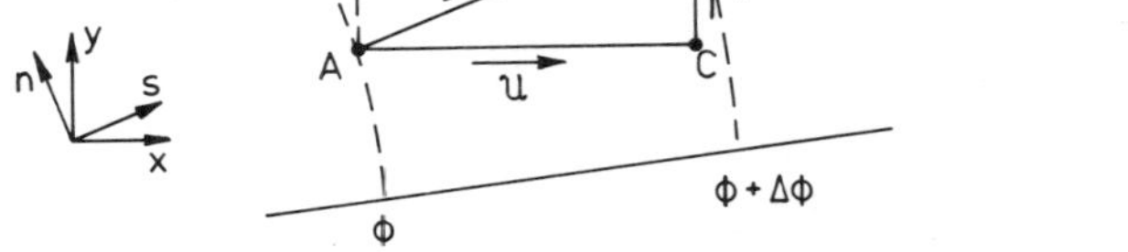

Figure 2.4 Velocities and circulation

We could now construct a series of lines of equal ϕ value, called equipotentials, for our two simple flows. Taking $\Delta\phi = \Delta\psi$ we get the patterns shown in Figure 2.5.

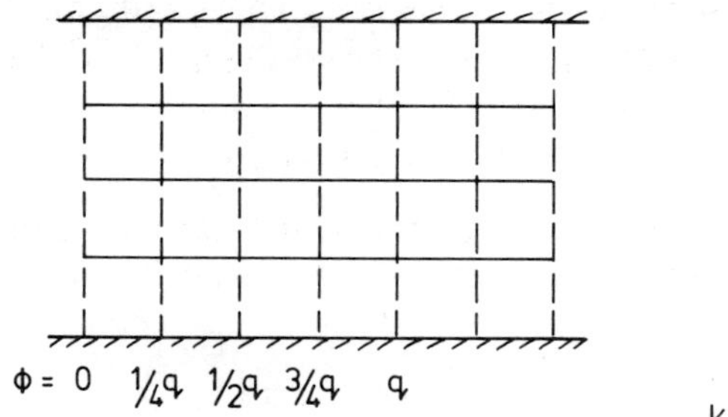

Figure 2.5 Velocity potential in uniform and converging flows

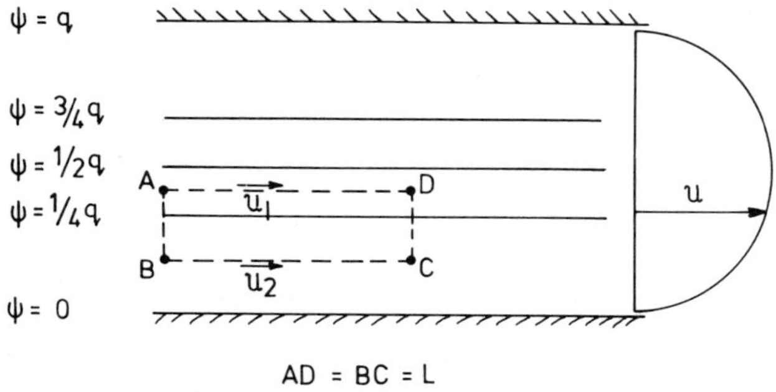

Figure 2.6 Friction and rotational flow

Notice that the pattern of equipotentials forms squares or curved 'squares' with the streamlines. Notice that we can only define ϕ sensibly in this way because the flow is frictionless and the velocity is equal across the channel. If the velocity was smaller at the edges of the channel ϕ would have different values at the same point if calculated by different paths, e.g. Figure 2.6.

$$\begin{aligned} &\text{via AD} && \phi_D = u_1 L \\ &\text{via ABCD} && \phi_D = 0 \times AB + u_2 L + 0 \times CD \\ & && \phi_D = u_2 L \end{aligned}$$

A general way of expressing the condition for ϕ to have a single value can be seen from Figure 2.4, if we say

$$\Delta\phi \text{ calculated via AB} = \Delta\phi \text{ via ABC}$$

i.e.

$$\Delta\phi = \frac{\partial \phi}{\partial y}(-\Delta y) + \frac{\partial \phi}{\partial x}\Delta x$$

This will always be true if we make

$$u = \frac{\partial \phi}{\partial x}, \quad v = \frac{\partial \phi}{\partial y}$$

and insist that

$$V\Delta s = u(-\Delta y) + v\Delta x$$

That is, the integral of tangential velocity × distance round a fluid element is zero. This quantity is called circulation Γ. It obviously indicates how fast the fluid in an element is spinning round. Hence when $\Gamma = 0$ for each element we call the flow irrotational. We must have irrotational flow for the velocity potential ϕ to exist. Another way of expressing this is to calculate Γ round a rectangular path such as ACBD in Figure 2.4

$$\Gamma = u\Delta x + (v + \frac{\partial v}{\partial x}\Delta x)(-\Delta y)$$

$$-(u - \frac{\partial u}{\partial y} - \Delta y)\Delta x - v(-\Delta y)$$

$$\Gamma = (-\frac{\partial u}{\partial y} + \frac{\partial v}{\partial x})\Delta y \Delta x$$

The quantity $-(\partial u/\partial y)+(\partial v/\partial x)$ is called vorticity, ω. For irrotational flow $\omega=0$. ω represents twice the angular velocity of a fluid particle.

2.3 Flow nets

The potential ϕ can be imagined as a surface from which the velocity is easily obtained. Velocity is the slope of the potential surface. Equipotentials are like contours giving the height of the surface. For the velocities to be 'downhill' we need to amend our definitions to

$$V=\frac{-\partial\phi}{\partial s},\quad u=\frac{-\partial\phi}{\partial x},\quad v=\frac{-\partial\phi}{\partial y} \tag{2.4}$$

$$V=\frac{-\partial\psi}{\partial n},\quad u=\frac{-\partial\psi}{\partial y},\quad v=\frac{+\partial\psi}{\partial x} \tag{2.5}$$

In the case of seepage flow, as we shall see later, the potential does correspond to a physical quantity. It is the total head, and velocities are related to its gradient by Darcy's law, which has the same form as Equation 2.4. Irrotational flow then allows us to define a velocity potential ϕ such that the equipotential lines form squares with the streamlines, when $\Delta\phi=\Delta\psi$.

This property of forming flow nets is extremely useful because it allows us to represent a potential flow by any pattern of lines having this feature of forming 'squares'; that is, lines which intersect at right angles and have equal spacing $\Delta n=\Delta s$ at each point. For example, suppose we wish to find the flow in a passage between two walls formed by circular arcs. We may suspect that more flow takes the shorter path round the inside of the bend but the exact distribution of velocity is not obvious. However, we have a pattern of 'squares' which will fit this case. If we take the flow net from Figure 2.5, the flow between converging walls, then all that is required is to swap the streamlines with equipotentials and the flow represents that in Figure 2.7. Velocities will now be along circular streamlines and have the value

$$V=\frac{\text{Constant}}{2\pi r} \tag{2.6}$$

Flows between more complicated boundaries can be found by simply finding a net of 'squares' which fits the boundary shape at the edges. There are several methods of doing this. Most obvious is the

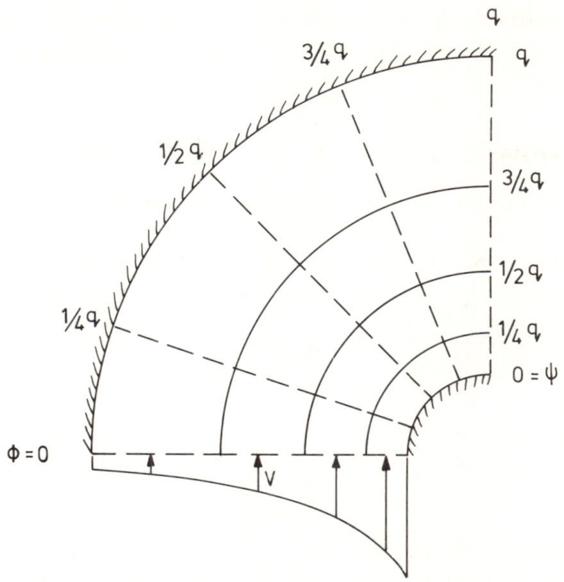

Figure 2.7 Flow net for a circular passage

method of sketching a flow net; then there is the method of combining patterns; also the method of systematically distorting or 'mapping' a known flow net; and finally the numerical methods. We shall briefly describe the first three methods and leave the numerical methods to the next chapter.

2.4 Sketching flow nets

This is simply a question of drawing the fixed flow boundaries to scale and adjusting the internal mesh until the best set of 'squares' has been formed. Usually it is easiest to draw the fixed outer ψ and ϕ lines, to sketch a few (two or three) internal ψ lines and then fit in as many ϕ lines as needed to make the squares. The sketched flow net will give a better qualitative idea of the flow than can be gained simply by looking at the shape. This is especially so in seepage problems where the seepage flow rate can be related to the overall head drop from the ratio of the number of flow passages to equipotential intervals in the flow net. A very accurate flow net would be needed to give the velocities in irrotational flow for determining pressure, and there is also the problem of defining the flow boundaries for a body in a very wide stream. This is where other methods are useful.

2.5 Combining simple solutions

We can show that a solution to the equation of potential flow will be obtained by adding several other solutions because this equation is linear.

Taking the definitions of ψ

$$u = \frac{\partial\psi}{\partial y}, \quad v = \frac{-\partial\psi}{\partial x}$$

and putting these in the irrotational flow condition

$$\frac{-\partial u}{\partial y} + \frac{\partial v}{\partial x} = 0$$

we have

$$\frac{\partial^2\psi}{\partial y^2} = \frac{\partial^2\psi}{\partial x^2} = 0 \tag{2.5}$$

The same equation applies for velocity potential ϕ. This is the equation for potential flow, Laplace's equation, which also governs heat conduction, magnetic and electric fields, etc.

The equation is linear and so we can indeed use the method of adding solutions. For example, if

$$\psi_1 = \psi_2 + \psi_3$$

$$\frac{\partial^2\psi_1}{\partial x^2} + \frac{\partial^2\psi_1}{\partial y^2} = \frac{\partial^2\psi_2}{\partial x^2} + \frac{\partial^2\psi_2}{\partial y^2} + \frac{\partial^2\psi_3}{\partial x^2} + \frac{\partial^2\psi_3}{\partial y^2}$$
$$= 0$$

if ψ_2 and ψ_3 satisfy Laplace's equation.

As an example of this let us take the flow in a straight channel and add it to the flow in a converging channel, letting the flow be from the narrow end this time. The flow in the straight channel is $8\,m^3/s/m$ depth and in the converging channel $4\,m^3/s$ so the stream functions for each separately will be as shown in Figure 2.8.

The dotted lines show streamlines for the combined flow, where ψ adds together from each simple flow to form a constant value in the new flow. Two of these streamlines of the new flow can be taken as boundaries of the new solution, which could represent flow in a channel shaped as shown in Figure 2.9.

Alternatively, the two simple solutions can be taken as far

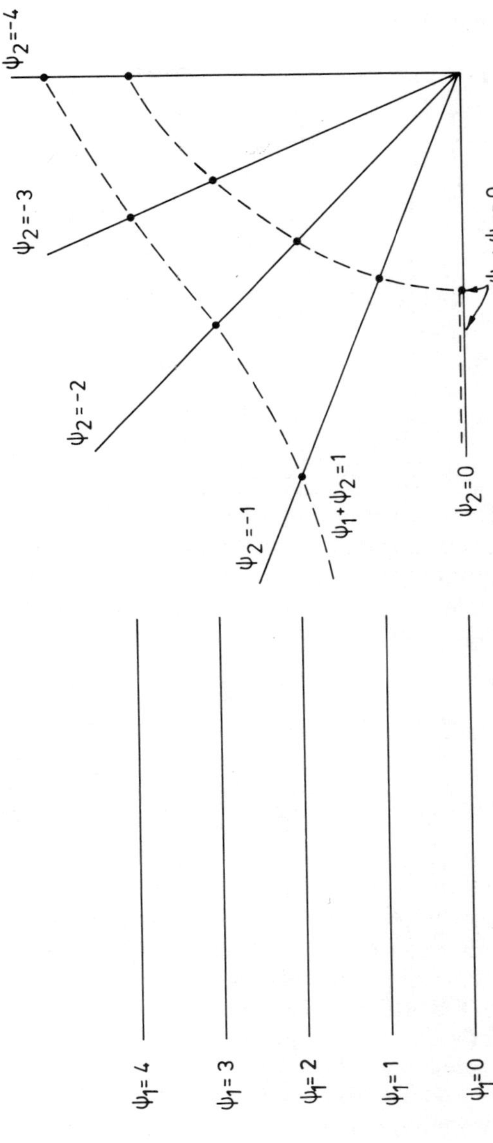

Figure 2.8 Combination of two flow patterns

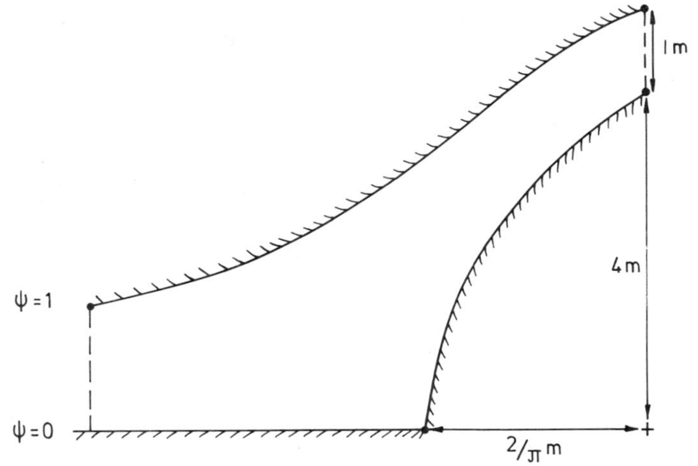

Figure 2.9 Possible boundaries for the flow of Figure 2.8

sideways as desired and the streamline $\psi = 0$ can be taken to represent a body in a very wide stream.

Extending our simple flow from a diverting channel by increasing the angle between the two sides results in a pattern known as a 'source' if the flow is outwards, or a 'sink' if the flow is inwards.

The potential flow function for these is

$$\psi = \frac{\theta q}{2\pi} \tag{2.6}$$

$$\phi = \frac{q}{2\pi} \ln r$$

where q = total flow from source (<0 for a sink).

The patterns produced by adding a stream and a number of sources or sinks can be investigated by calculating the combined value of ψ from the simple solutions at a number of positions and interpolating to find the positions of the streamlines. If we are interested in the flow round a body in a stream the position of the line $\psi = 0$, representing the body surface, is particularly relevant.

The sum of a source and a sink of equal flow with a stream will be found to represent a closed body similar to an ellipse in shape. As the source and sink are brought closer together the shape becomes more circular. The flow from the source and into the sink has to be increased to maintain the same size of body of course. It can be shown that the flow due to a source and a sink very close together is a doublet, conveniently represented by the complex number

$$W = \phi + \mathbf{i}\,\psi = \frac{m}{(x + \mathbf{i}y)} = \frac{m}{z} \tag{2.7}$$

This follows from expressing the source and sink in complex form as

$$\phi + \mathbf{i}\,\psi = \frac{q}{2\pi} \ln z = \frac{q}{2\pi} \ln re^{\mathrm{i}\theta}$$

$$\text{(so that } \phi + \mathbf{i}\,\psi = \frac{q}{2\pi} (\ln r + \mathbf{i}\theta) \text{ as before)}$$

Then a source plus a sink is

$$\begin{aligned}
\phi + \mathbf{i}\,\psi &= \frac{q}{2\pi} \ln z_1 - \ln z_2 \\
&= \frac{q}{2\pi} \ln (z - z_a) - \ln (z - z_b) \\
&= \frac{q}{2\pi} \ln \left(\frac{z - z_a}{z - z_b} \right) = \ln \frac{1}{1 + \dfrac{\Delta}{z - z_a}} \\
&\simeq \frac{q}{2\pi} \left[-\ln \left(1 - \frac{\Delta}{z} \right) \right] \\
&\simeq \frac{q\Delta}{2\pi} \left[\left(\frac{1}{z} \right) + \text{etc.} \right]
\end{aligned}$$

Hence, taking $q\Delta/2\pi = m =$ constant gives the result above.

Now, adding the complex potential for a stream

$$w = U_0 z = U_0 (x + \mathbf{i}y)$$

we get

$$w = U_0 z + \frac{m}{z}$$

For $\psi = 0$, $r = a$ we want

$$\psi = \text{imag.} \left(U_0\, ae^{\mathrm{i}\theta} + \frac{m}{ae^{\mathrm{i}\theta}} \right) = 0$$

i.e.

$$m = -U_0 a^2$$

$$w = U_0\left(z + \frac{a^2}{z}\right) \tag{2.8}$$

So, e.g.

$$\psi = \text{imag.}\left(U_0\left(re^{i\theta} + \frac{a^2}{re^{i\theta}}\right)\right)$$

$$\psi = U_0 r \sin\theta - \frac{a^2}{r}\sin\theta$$

This function now represents the flow round a circular cylinder in a stream.

2.6 Mapping

The use of complex numbers allows another method of solution for potential flows. Any function of a complex variable (with some provisos) represents a mapping of shapes from one complex plane to another. Furthermore, this mapping leaves the shapes in each small region the same although the relative sizes of regions change gradually. So flow nets will remain as flow nets after being mapped. For example, take the mapping shown in Figure 2.10

$$Z = \ln z$$
$$X + Y = \ln r + i\theta \tag{2.9}$$

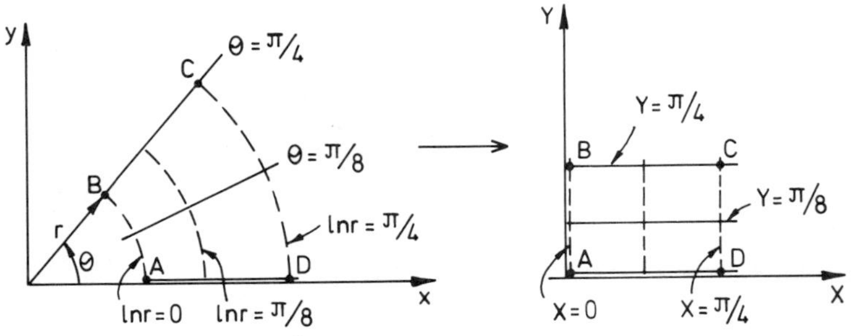

Figure 2.10 Example of mapping a flow net

Radial lines (const. θ) become lines of constant Y, and circles of radius r become lines of constant X. The flow net for a source has been mapped into that for a stream.

The process of mapping could perhaps be imagined as drawing a flow net on a rubber sheet and then stretching parts of the sheet so that the boundaries of the flow net take on a different shape. If we are still left with a pattern of curved 'squares' inside the boundaries then we have the solution to the flow between the new boundaries. This can be seen particularly in the case of the transformation

$$Z = z + \frac{1}{z} \tag{2.10}$$

A circle of radius 1 centred at (0,0) is mapped into a flat shape from −2 to +2 in figure 2.11. We can see this since:

$$Y_1 = \left(1 - \frac{1}{1}\right) \sin\theta$$

$$X_1 = \left(1 + \frac{1}{1}\right) \cos\theta$$

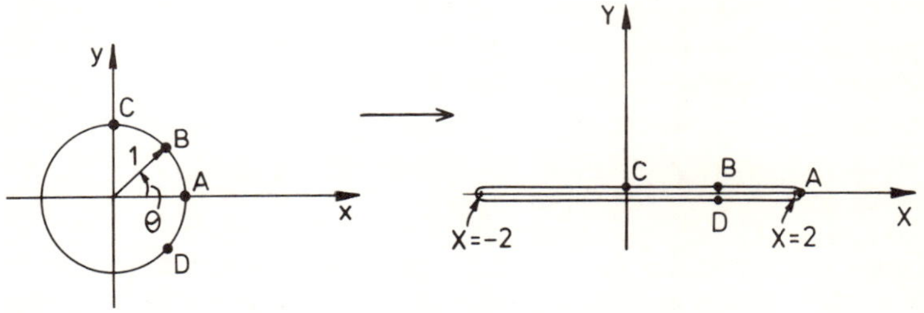

Figure 2.11 Mapping a circle to a flat shape

The effect is almost like pulling the ends of a diameter of a hole in a rubber sheet until the hole is flat. By the way, we can see that if a uniform stream flow net is sketched round the flattened shape so that $\phi = X$, $\psi = Y$, and then the mapping is followed back onto the circle, the expressions for ϕ and ψ on a circle are correctly obtained.

Many other shapes can be obtained by this mapping if circles of a radius other than 1 are taken and the centre of the circle is moved slightly from the origin. In particular, wing-like shapes can be easily produced, see Figure 2.12. Since the flow round a circle is known, the potential on any of these new shapes can be found. A point on the circle is chosen, its potential calculated, and this will be the same

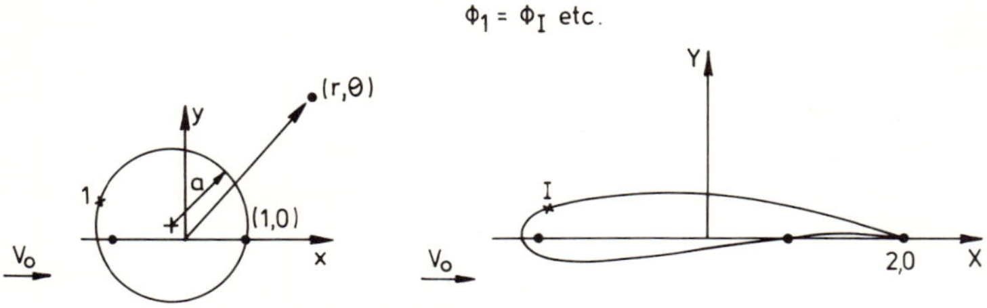

Figure 2.12 Mapping a circle to a wing shape

at the mapped point. Velocities round the new shape can be calculated from the new gradients of ϕ along the surface.

2.7 Bernoulli's equation

In frictionless potential flow the accelerations of the fluid are balanced by the pressures and the weight of the fluid. Take the flow in a converging channel, for example. A particle moving from the low velocity at A to the high velocity at B has accelerated. Assuming the flow is horizontal it must have been propelled by a pressure force in order to do this. The pressure must be lower at B than at A to achieve this, but what exactly is the relationship between pressure at A and at B?

We may decide this by analysing the motion of a fluid particle, as shown in Figure 2.13. Taking the force equation in the x-direction the pressure force on the particle is

$$F_p = \frac{\partial p}{\partial x} \times \text{Volume of particle}$$

This is similar to the hydrostatic force on a body in a fluid and may be seen by taking the particle as a number of tubes with axes in the x-direction.

The weight force is

$$F_W = \rho g \times \text{Volume} \times \frac{\partial h}{\partial x}$$

$\partial h/\partial x$ giving the component of total weight, ρg . Volume, in the x-direction. Then

$$\rho \,.\, \text{Volume} \frac{\mathrm{D}u}{\mathrm{D}t} = \frac{-\partial p}{\partial x} \text{Volume} + \rho g \,.\, \text{Volume} \frac{\partial h}{\partial x}$$

$$\frac{\mathrm{D}u}{\mathrm{D}t} = -\left(\frac{1}{\rho}\frac{\partial p}{\partial x} + g\frac{\partial h}{\partial x}\right) \qquad (2.12)$$

where

u = velocity in x-direction
p = pressure
ρ = density
h = height of a point (x,y) above some datum

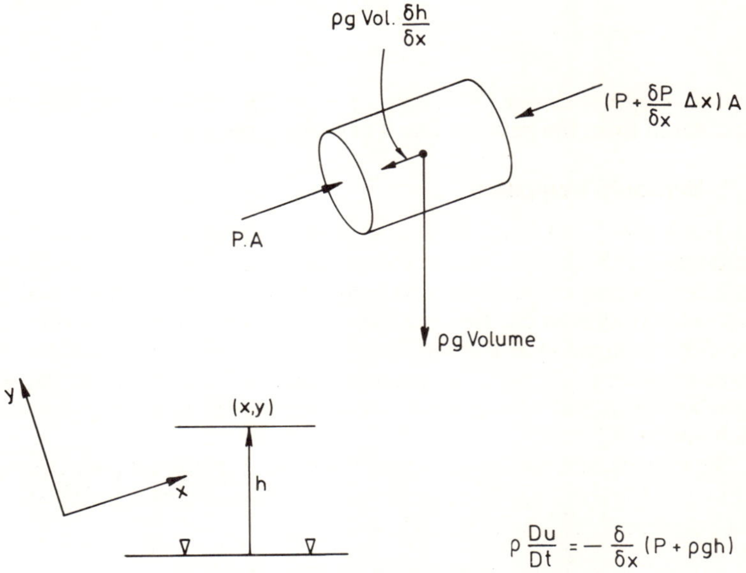

Figure 2.13 Definitions for Bernoulli's equation

Du/Dt is the total acceleration of the particle. Even if the velocities at fixed points do not change with time Du/Dt will have a value different from zero. We work in a system where velocities are known at fixed points in space (called the Eulerian system). We must now find Du/Dt in terms of these velocities. Suppose our fluid particle moves from x, y to $(x+\Delta x, y+\Delta y)$ where the velocity in the x-direction is $u+(\partial u/\partial x)\,\Delta x+(\partial u/\partial y)\,\Delta y$. If this occurs in a time Δt

$$\frac{Du}{Dt}=\left(u+\frac{\partial u}{\partial x}\Delta x+\frac{\partial u}{\partial y}\Delta y-u\right)\Big/\Delta t$$

$$\frac{Du}{Dt}=u\frac{\partial u}{\partial x}+v\frac{\partial u}{\partial y} \tag{2.13}$$

If the velocities are also changing with time as well as with x, y, as in Figure 2.14

$$\frac{Du}{Dt} = \frac{\partial u}{\partial t} + u\frac{\partial u}{\partial x} + v\frac{\partial u}{\partial y} \qquad (2.14)$$

The equation for pressure would now be

$$\frac{\partial p}{\partial x} = \rho\left(\frac{\partial u}{\partial t} + u\frac{\partial u}{\partial x} + v\frac{\partial u}{\partial u} + g\frac{\partial h}{\partial x}\right) \qquad (2.15)$$

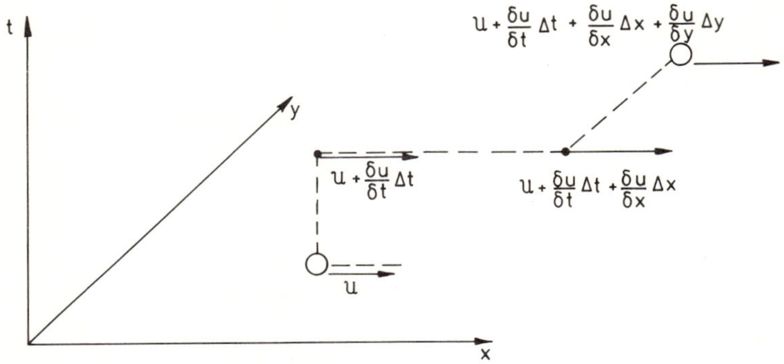

Figure 2.14 Definitions for total acceleration

This, and the equation in the *y*-direction for $\partial p/\partial y$, could be integrated to find the pressure at a point B, starting from point A. However, we can simplify this integration by using some results from potential flow. Since the flow is irrotational

$$\frac{-\partial u}{\partial y} + \frac{\partial v}{\partial x} = 0$$

and u can be related to velocity potential by $u \equiv \partial\phi/\partial x$.

Using these in Equation 2.15 gives

$$\frac{\partial}{\partial x}\left(\frac{p}{\rho} + \frac{u^2 + v^2}{2} + gh + \frac{\partial\phi}{\partial t}\right) = 0 \qquad (2.16)$$

and a similar equation in the *y*-direction can be derived. To find the pressure at any point we need only to integrate these from a point 0 where p_0 etc. are known. We find:

$$\frac{p}{\rho} + \frac{u^2 + v^2}{2} + gh + \frac{\partial\phi}{\partial t} = \frac{p_0}{\rho} + \frac{u_0^{\,2} + v_0^{\,2}}{2} + gh_0 + \frac{\partial\phi_0}{\partial t} \qquad (2.17)$$

This is Bernoulli's equation for an unsteady potential flow.

2.8 Application of Bernoulli's equation

Bernoulli's equation is used to find pressures in steady and unsteady potential flow. Sometimes the pressure is needed in its own right, for example to check whether cavitation is likely, and sometimes as a step towards calculating force on the whole or part of a surface. We can illustrate this by a number of examples, which will also show some general results on forces experienced by a body in potential flow.

2.9 Pressure in a circular passage

This could form the crest of a siphon spillway, shown in Figure 2.15.

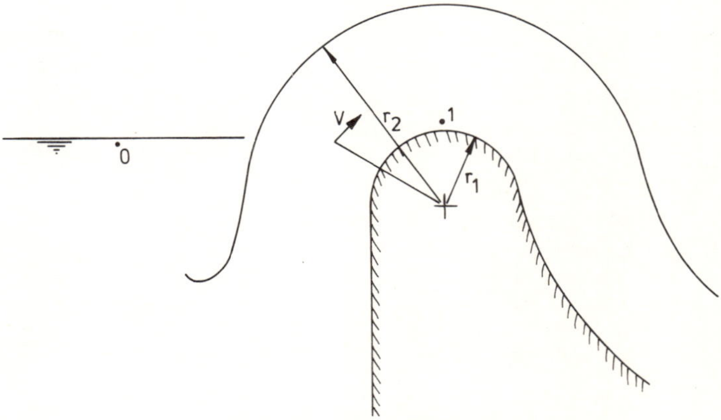

Figure 2.15 Flow through a siphon

The velocity will be seen to be greatest at the point 1 on the inside of the curved passage. This velocity can be related to the flow through the passage by the expression for the potential flow

$$V = \frac{\Gamma}{2\pi r}$$

$$q = \psi_2 - \psi = \frac{\Gamma}{2\pi} \ln \frac{r_2}{r_1}$$

so

$$V = \frac{q}{\ln \dfrac{r_2}{r_1}} \cdot \frac{1}{r}$$

Using Bernoulli's equation

$$p_1 = p_0 + \tfrac{1}{2}\rho V_0^2 + \rho g z_0 + \frac{\partial \phi_0}{\partial t}$$

$$- \left(\tfrac{1}{2}\rho\, V_1^2 + \rho g z_1 + \frac{\partial \phi}{\partial t} \right)$$

For a steady flow $\partial\phi/\partial t = 0$, and for $z_0 = z_1$, $p_0 = 0$ and $V_0 = 0$

$$p_1 = \tfrac{1}{2}\rho\, V_1^2 = \tfrac{1}{2}\rho \left(\frac{q}{\ln \dfrac{r_2}{r_1}} \cdot \frac{1}{r} \right)^2$$

If the limit on p_1 is that it must be greater than the vapour pressure, we can work out the maximum flow rate per unit width q. The forces tending to collapse the siphon could also be examined by finding pressures on the walls at other points.

2.10 Forces on a circle with a circulation

The potential flow solution for the velocities on a circular cylinder in a stream which also has a circulation Γ round it (see Figure 2.16) are found from

$$u = \frac{1}{r}\,\frac{\partial}{\partial \theta}\,(\phi) - \frac{\Gamma}{2\pi a}$$

$$= \frac{1}{a}\;U_0 2a \sin\theta - \frac{\Gamma}{2\pi a}$$

$$= 2\;U_0 \sin\theta - \frac{\Gamma}{2\pi a}$$

Using Bernoulli's equation to find the pressure on the surface of the cylinder

$$p = p_0 + \tfrac{1}{2}\rho\; U_0^2 - \tfrac{1}{2}\rho u^2$$

$$u^2 = (2U_0 \sin\theta)^2 - 2\left(2\;U_0 \sin\theta\;\frac{\Gamma}{2\pi a} \right) + \left(\frac{\Gamma}{2\pi a} \right)^2$$

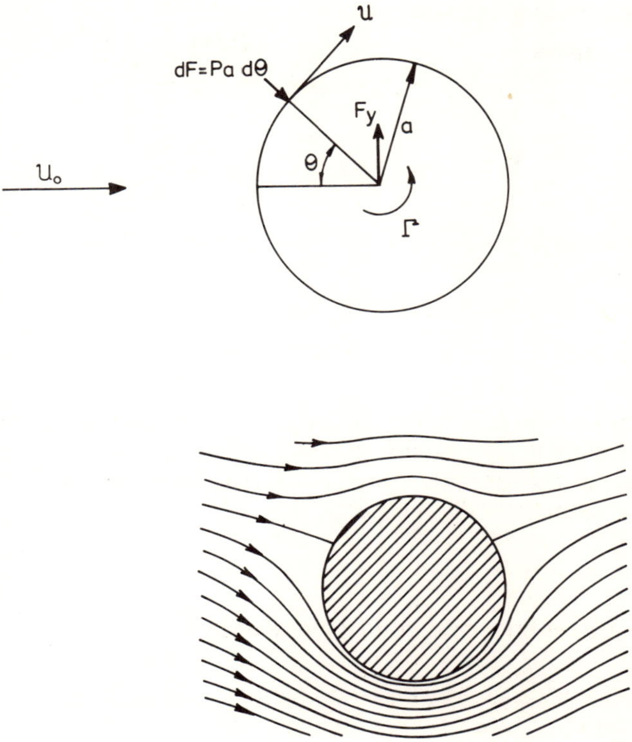

Figure 2.16 Flow round a cylinder with circulation

The force in line with the stream will be zero because there are equal p terms at equal y values on the front and rear faces. The force across the stream can be found from

$$F_y = -\int_0^{2\pi} p \sin\theta \, a \, d\theta$$

Substituting for the pressure we have

$$F_y = -\int_0^{2\pi} \left[p_0 + \tfrac{1}{2}\rho U_0^2 - \tfrac{1}{2}\rho \left(4\, U_0^2 \sin^2\theta - 2U_0 \sin\theta \frac{\Gamma}{\pi a} + \frac{\Gamma^2}{4\pi^2 a^2} \right) \right] a \sin\theta \, d\theta$$

Now many of the terms integrate to zero since

$$\int_0^{2\pi} \sin^n \theta \, d\theta = 0 \text{ for } n \text{ odd}$$

so

$$F_y = -\rho \, U_0 \frac{\Gamma}{\pi} \int_0^{2\pi} \sin^2 \theta d\theta$$

$$F_y = -\rho U_0 \Gamma \qquad (2.18)$$

This remarkably simple result also holds for any other shape in potential flow.

2.11 Expression for pressures and forces

The pressures p are often expressed as a pressure coefficient

$$C_p = (p - p_0)/\tfrac{1}{2} \rho U_0^2 \qquad (2.19)$$

So in a steady flow

$$C_p = (p_0 + \tfrac{1}{2} p u_0^2 - \tfrac{1}{2} \rho V^2 - p_0)/^{1/2} \rho U_0^2$$

$$C_p = 1 - \frac{V^2}{U_0^2} \qquad (2.20)$$

V = resultant velocity.

The force on a body is then found by integrating the pressures over the surface, so

$$F_x = \int_C p ds \cos \theta$$

$$F_y = -\int_C p ds \sin \theta$$

where C = curve of body shape
θ = angle between normal to body surface and x-direction
ds = distance along the surface.

Where the points on the body are specified, these equations can be expressed as

$$F_x = \sum_{i=1}^{NP} p_i \Delta y_i \, , \, F_y = \sum_{i=1}^{NP} p_i \Delta x_i$$

where NP = number of points.

Like pressures, forces are usually expressed as coefficients

$$C_X = \frac{F_x}{\tfrac{1}{2}\rho U_0^2 DL}$$
$$C_y = \frac{F_y}{\tfrac{1}{2}\rho U_0^2 DL} \qquad (2.21)$$

where D = *width of body*
L = length at right angles to plane of flow (usually 1.0).

If x is also the stream direction then the drag coefficient $C_D = C_X$ and the lift coefficient $C_L = C_Y$.

2.12 Boundary layer on a flat plate

Potential flows were described as being those flows where friction played little part in determining the overall flow pattern. It was assumed that flows over streamlined bodies, for example, could be calculated by potential flow theory because the effects of friction were confined to a small layer of fluid close to the body. This is the boundary layer. One of the results of potential flow theory was that no force on a body in line with the stream is predicted. There must of course be some force due to frictional effects and to calculate this we must include the boundary layer in our calculations. The actual size of the boundary layer can be found and our assumption that it was small can be checked.

To gain some idea of the boundary layer, imagine that a very thin plate is introduced into a uniform stream as in Figure 2.17, parallel to the stream. The potential flow solution must apply quite close to the plate since it offers very little disturbance to the original pattern of flow. However, fluid very close to the plate must be slowed by contact with the surface of the plate or slower moving layers of fluid below it. Thus a region of slower moving rotational fluid is established next to the plate and grows thicker in the downstream direction. Outside this region, the boundary layer, the original potential flow solution will still apply. It will be seen that changes in velocity of the fluid occurs very rapidly as the layer is crossed. For example, fluid has zero velocity immediately next to the plate and the full stream velocity just outside the boundary layer. Along the length of the layer, however, change occurs very slowly. Fluid motion is predominantly in one direction, along the length of the layer, and so the pressure just outside the layer applies all the way across the thin boundary layer. These characteristics mean that the

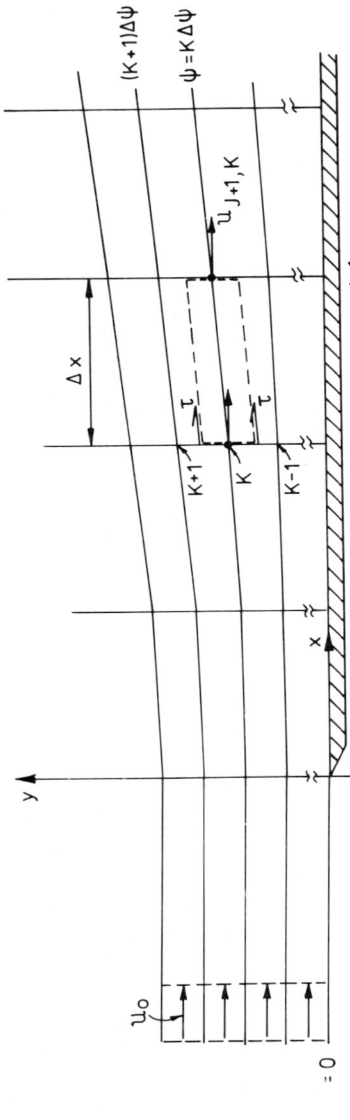

Figure 2.17 Boundary layer flow

boundary layer can be described by equations which are simpler than the full equations of flow.

By using the streamlines of the flow as one coordinate, instead of the physical distance y, a simple equation can be derived for the velocity U in the x-direction. To do this we apply the momentum equation to a small control volume of unit depth normal to the flow such as the one shown by dotted lines in Figure 2.17.

Forces on fluid = Rate of increase of momentum in passing through control volume

Note that the flow rate through the control volume is 1.0 $\Delta\psi$. The frictional force is given by the difference in shear stress τ on the top and bottom faces times the area of these faces. This area is $1.0 \times \Delta x$ if the flow is nearly parallel to the x-direction as assumed for the boundary layer. Finally, the area of the end face of the control volume $\Delta y_{J,K} \times 1.0$ is $1.0 \times \Delta\psi / U_{J,K}$. This is approximately equal to $1.0 \times \Delta y_{j+1/2,K}$ if the steps are small. The momentum equation thus becomes

$$-\frac{dp}{dx}\frac{\Delta\psi}{U_{J,K}} + (\tau_{J,K+1/2} - \tau_{J,K-1/2})\Delta x = \rho\Delta\psi(U_{J+1,K} - U_{J,K})$$

This can be written

$$U_{J+1,K} = U_{J,K} + \frac{\Delta x}{\rho\Delta\psi}(\tau_{J,K+1/2} - \tau_{J,K-1/2}) - \frac{\delta p}{dx}\frac{1}{\rho U_{J,K}} \tag{2.22}$$

So that if τ can be related to U, downstream values of U can be calculated from a known set of upstream values. The solution for the whole boundary layer can be found by 'marching' downstream.

This is achieved by using the relationship between the shear stress and velocity gradient for a laminar flow

$$\tau = \mu\frac{\partial u}{\partial y}$$

i.e.

$$\tau_{J,K+1/2} = \mu\frac{(U_{J,K+1} - U_{J,K})}{\Delta y_{J,K+1/2}} \tag{2.23}$$

where μ = viscosity of fluid.

The definition of ψ can also be used to give

$$\Delta y_{J,K+1/2} = \frac{\Delta\psi}{(U_{J,K+1} + U_{J,K})/2} \tag{2.24}$$

Finally, for a flat plate parallel to a stream the velocity at the edge of the layer is always U_0, so by Bernoulli's equation p is constant and $dp/dx = 0$. This gives an equation for the velocity

$$U_{J+1,K} = U_{J,K} + \frac{\mu\Delta x}{2\rho\Delta\psi^2}(U^2_{J,K+1} + U^2_{J,K-1} - 2\,U^2_{J,K}) \tag{2.25}$$

By dividing the boundary layer up into a number of steps across the layer, the velocity profile can be represented by a number of point values and the profile at a small distance Δx downstream calculated using Equation 2.25. The process can then be repeated to 'march' downstream.

An exact solution to the problem was found by Blasius and this gives the thickness of the boundary layer δ as

$$\frac{\delta}{x} = \frac{5}{\sqrt{\left(\frac{U_0\,x}{\nu}\right)}} \tag{2.26}$$

where δ = value of y for which $U = 0.99\,U_0$
ν = kinematic viscosity of fluid.

The shear stress at the surface of the plate is given by

$$\frac{\tau_0}{\rho U_0^2} = \frac{0.644}{\sqrt{\left(\frac{U_0\,x}{\nu}\right)}} \tag{2.27}$$

These can be deduced from Blasius' solution for U/U_0 as a function of $Y\sqrt{(U_0/\nu x)}$ shown in Figure 2.18.

2.13 Bibliography

1. Douglas, J. F., Gasiorek, J. M. and Swaffield, J. A., *Fluid Mechanics,* Pitman (1979).
2. Massy, B. S., *Mechanics of Fluids,* 5th edition, Van Nostrand Reinhold (1983).
3. Milne-Thomson, L. M., *Theoretical Hydrodynamics,* 5th Edition Macmillan (1968).
4. Lamb, H., *Hydrodynamics,* 6th Edition, Cambridge University Press (1932).
5. Kirchoff, R. H., *Potential Flows,* Marcel Dekker (1985).

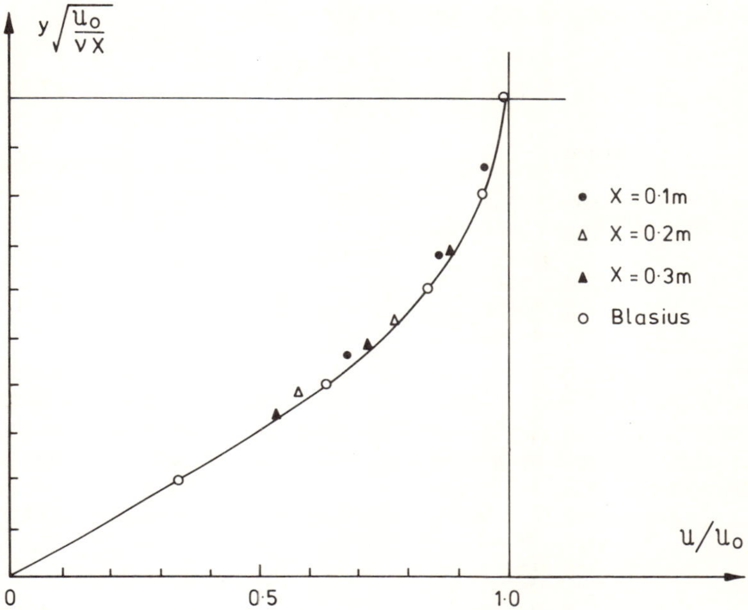

Figure 2.18 Velocities in a laminar boundary layer on a flat plate

WORKED EXAMPLES

Example 2.1 XYSP1: stream function and potential in a source

A short program to calculate the stream function and velocity potential of a source is given below. The program is straightforward except in the calculation of θ (called T1). Since BASIC returns a value of θ between $-\pi/2$ and $\pi/2$ from the function ATN(x), the angle $T2 = \theta - \pi/2$ is found from $T2 = ATN\ (\Delta x/\Delta y)$, and then $\theta = T1 = T2 + \pi/2$, or if $\Delta y = 0$, $\theta = T2 + 3\pi/2$. This also keeps the jump in ϕ along the line $\theta = 2\pi$. With this program the values of ψ and ϕ at points on a reference grid can be found and the incompressible continuity equation and irrotational flow condition checked. Also the stream lines and equipotentials of the flow can be found by searching for points of constant ψ. For example, finding ψ at the points given below, for a source of unit strength ($q/2\pi = 1.0$) at (0,0):

x	0	0	0	0.1	−0.1
y	1	1.1	0.9	1	1
ψ	−1.5708	−1.5708	1.5708	−1.6704	−1.4711
Name	P	N	S	E	W

The circulation about the central point (0,1) is:

$$\Gamma_p = [-(\psi_N + \psi_S + \psi_E + \psi_W) + 4\,\psi_p] = 0$$

Program XYSP1

```
100  INPUT "X POINT";XP
110  INPUT "Y POINT";YP
120  INPUT "X SOURCE";XS
130  INPUT "Y SOURCE";YS
140  INPUT "Q/2PI SOURCE";QS
150 DX = XP - XS
160 DY = YP - YS
170 RS = DX ^ 2 + DY ^ 2
180 T2 =  ATN (DX / DY)
190 T1 = T2 + 1.5708
200  IF DY < 0 THEN T1 = T2 + 4.7124
210 SP =  - QS * T1
220 PP = QS *  LOG (RS) / 2
230  PRINT "STREAM FUNC.= ";SP
240  PRINT "VEL. POT.= ";PP
250  INPUT "ENTER 1 TO REPEAT- ";NR
260  IF NR = 1 GOTO 100
270  STOP
```

Program notes

(1) From line 100 to 140 the position of a point, the source and the source strength are input. XP and YP are the coordinates of the point where ψ, stream function, and ϕ, velocity potential, are calculated. XS and YS are the coordinates of the source and QS is the strength of the source ($q/2\pi$).
(2) Lines 150 to 220 calculate ψ and ϕ at point P. Lines 150 to 170 calculate the distance RS from the source S, to the point P. Lines 180 to 200 find the angle between the horizontal and the line from S to P. Lines 190 to 200 are required because the function ATN returns a value between $+\pi$ and $-\pi$. The stream function SP and potential PP are calculated from the potential flow functions for a source

$$\psi = \frac{q}{2\pi}\,\theta,\ \phi = \frac{q}{2\pi}\ln r$$

(3) In lines 230 to 260 the stream function and velocity potential are printed and an option is given to repeat the calculation for a further point. The program stops at line 270.

Example 2.2 Splot: streamlines of sources and a stream

A program, SPLOT, for finding the streamlines due to a stream and a number of sources (or sinks), follows. The program finds the value of stream function ψ at points on a grid and then finds the height at which a given value of ψ occurs on each column of the grid. Line 100 reserves storage for the ψ values on a (21 ×21) grid and also the strength and x coordinates of up to 10 sources. Lines 110–140 are concerned with input, as indicated by the listing. Lines 150 and 160 set the scaling factor SF for the plotting. The ψ values are found in lines 250 to 310. Line 255 is included to reassure the user that the program is running! Line 350 calls the subroutine to plot the streamlines, which starts at line 1000. HOME cleans the screen, VTAB24 sets the cursor at the bottom of the screen and HGR brings the graphics routines into operation. The number of ψ lines and the interval $\Delta\psi$ between each is input in lines 1040 and 1041. For each ψ value the columns of the grid are searched for its y location assuming a linear variation in ψ between the nodes. These y points in each column are joined by straight lines using the instruction HPLOT X_1, Y_1 (line 1140) to mark a point in the first column and then HPLOT TO X_1, Y_1 (line 1160) to join following points by drawing to that point.

The sources are all situated on the x-axis in this program since it makes the program shorter and avoids the double value of ψ that would occur for $\theta = 2\pi$. Take as a first example a 20 × 10 grid with a stream of 1.0 m/s and source of strength $q/2\pi = 1.0\,m^2/s$ at $x = 5$. Then if five stream lines are plotted at intervals $\Delta\psi = 1.0$ the flow apparently is diverted round an obstacle which is represented by the source. Plotting one streamline with a small interval, say $\Delta\psi = 0.01$, reveals the shape of the obstacle more clearly.

If a source with a strength of -1.0 is added at $x = 10$, we see that the flow round a finite body is modelled. Increasing the strengths of the sources and bringing them closer together produces a more circular shape.

Program SPLOT

```
100  DIM S(21,21),QS(10),XS(10)
110  INPUT "NO. GRID COLS.?";J2
111  INPUT "NO. GRID ROWS? ";K2
112  INPUT "STREAM VELOCITY?";U1
113  INPUT "NO. SOURCES?";M1
120  FOR M = 1 TO M1
130  INPUT "Q/2PI? ";QS(M)
131  INPUT "X?     ";XS(M)
```

```
140  NEXT M
150 SF = 160 / K2
160  IF SF > 360 / J2 THEN SF = 360 / J2
250  FOR J = 1 TO J2
255  PRINT "ROW ";J;" OF ";J2
260  FOR K = 2 TO K2
270 S(J,K) = U1 * (K - 1)
280  FOR M = 1 TO M1
285 T1 = (J - XS(M)) / (K - 1)
290 T1 =  ATN (T1) + 1.5708
295 S(J,K) = S(J,K) + QS(M) * T1
300  NEXT M
310  NEXT K: NEXT J
350  GOSUB 1000
352  INPUT "TO REPLOT ENTER 1-";NR
354  IF NR = 1 GOTO 350
500  STOP
1000  REM  PLOTS STREAMLINES
1010  HOME
1020  VTAB 24
1030  HGR
1040  INPUT "NO. STREAMLINES?";NSL
1041  INPUT "INTERVAL BETWEEN LINES?";DS
1050  FOR I = 1 TO NSL
1060 S1 = DS * I:K = 0
1070  FOR J = 1 TO J2
1075 DY = 0
1080 K = K + 1
1085  IF K = K2 GOTO 1110
1090  IF S(J,K) < S1 GOTO 1080
1100 DY = (S(J,K) - S1) / (S(J,K) - S(J,K - 1))
1110 Y1 = (K2 - K + DY) * SF
1120 X1 = J * SF
1130  IF J > 1 GOTO 1160
1140  HPLOT X1,Y1
1150  GOTO 1170
1160  HPLOT  TO X1,Y1
1170 K = 0
1175  NEXT J: NEXT I
1180  RETURN
```

Program notes

(1) Line 100 sets up arrays for the stream function S(21, 21) on a grid of 21 × 21 points and smaller arrays for 10 sources. WS(10) gives the source strength of $(q/2\pi)$ and XS(10) the x-coordinate. The sources are assumed to lie on the x-axis.

(2) Lines 110 to 113 input the number of grid columns, J2, and rows, K2. The stream velocity U1 and number of sources M1 are also input.

(3) Lines 120 to 140 form a loop where the source strength QS and x-coordinate are input for each source from 1 to M1.
(4) At lines 150 and 160 a scale factor SF is calculated so that the plot may fill the screen height of 160 pixels, and a width of 360 pixels.
(5) In lines 250 to 310 the stream function is calculated at each grid point. A message is printed at line 255 as each new column is started to inform the user of the progress of the calculation. At each point the contributions from the stream, line 270, and each source, lines 280 to 300, are added to find the total stream function value.
(6) At line 350 the plotting subroutine is entered and after this an option to repeat the plotting routine is offered before the end of the program.
(7) The plotting subroutine starts at line 1000; lines 1010 to 1030 set up the screen for plotting on the particular computer type used to develop this program.
(8) The number of streamlines, NSL, and the interval between each, DS, is then input in lines 1040 and 1041.
(9) In lines 1050 to 1175 there is a loop for each streamline. In line 1060 the stream function value, S1, on this line is calculated. The location of this value is then sought on each column of the grid in lines 1070 to 1100. K is the first grid row with a higher value than S1 and DY is the distance of the streamline below this point, assuming a linear variation between points.
(10) At line 1110 the vertical position on the screen is calculated, allowing for the downward numbering of pixels and the scale factor. The horizontal screen position is found in line 1120. If the first grid column is being dealt with line 1130 diverts the program to line 1160 so that a point is plotted. Otherwise line 1140 draws a line from the last point to the present one.
(11) Line 1170 resets the row number to zero for the search up the next column. After each column has been searched for the position of each streamline and the lines plotted, the routine returns to the main program at line 352.

Example 2.3 TRANC1: transforms circle flow and plots shape

The flow round a circle is given by Section 2.5 and Equation 2.8. A number of other shapes can be derived by this mapping, as explained in Section 2.6. In particular, the following transformation is given

$$w = z + \frac{1}{z}$$

with $w = u + iv$ now representing coordinates in the new u, v plane instead of ψ and ϕ. $z = x + iy$ is the position in the x, y plane where the circle flow takes place. By applying this transformation to various sizes of circles with their centres at different positions we can produce a variety of shapes, from a flat plate to a curved aerofoil. Since we know the solution for the flow round a circle we can also find the flow round these new shapes. The positions of streamlines and equipotentials are simply transformed by the same equation that we applied to the circle, and in particular the ϕ values on the surface of the new shape are the same as values at equivalent points on the circle. A program, called TRANC1, to display the shapes produced by transforming various circles and to calculate the velocities at points on the surface of the new shapes, is given below.

The program is largely self-explanatory and uses three subroutines to transform the circle to a new shape using Equation 2.16 to plot the new shape and then to work out the velocities on this shape. An example of a run of the program can be seen following the listing. A radius for the circle to be transformed is called for, and x, y coordinates for the centre, together with the number of points to be calculated. Entering the data RC = 1.25, XC = 0.25, YC = 0, NP = 20, produces the transformed coordinates, shown for the new shape. From these we can see that the shape lies between $x = +2.2$ and $x = -2.1$ and also between $y = +0.52$ and $y = -0.52$.

The program will plot this shape on the monitor screen when a scaling factor and additional values to the x and y values are supplied. These quantities are needed to fit the plot in an area from $x = 0$ to 360 and $y = 0$ to 160. Entering the values SF = 20, XS = 100, YS = 70 puts the shape in the area $x = 2.1 \times 20 + 100$ to $x = +2.2 \times 20 + 100$ and $y = -0.52 \times 20 + 70$ to $y = +0.52 \times 20 + 70$. From the plot in figure 2.19 we can see that the shape produced is like a wing with a sharp trailing edge. This sharp edge is produced when the original circle passes through the point $(-1,0)$ or $(+1,0)$. If we wish to find the velocities on the surface of this new shape we can enter any letter other than Y in response. The program assumes a unit stream velocity which can be directed at an angle AF (in radians) to the x-axis. Increasing AF is equivalent to increasing the incidence of the shape in a flow from Right to Left. A circulation can also be added to the flow, positive circulation being anticlockwise. In the example both the quantities AF and GC are taken as zero, and the velocities printed out are therefore symmetrical on the top and bottom surface of the shape. These velocities are at points halfway between the points whose coordinates were printed earlier in the program. They are calculated in the section of the program starting at line 3000, by finding the velocity potential on the circle and transferring these values to the transformed points. The velocities on the new shape are then found by calculating the potential gradients along the surface working in an anticlockwise direction round the shape. Having found potential and velocity we can work out the pressures as explained in the next section.

Program TRANC1

```
100  DIM X2(100),Y2(100),P2(100),V2(100
110  INPUT "RADIUS? ";RC
120  INPUT "X CENTRE? ";XC
130  INPUT "Y CENTRE? ";YC
140  INPUT "NO. OF POINTS? ";NP
145  PRINT "TRANSFORMING CIRCLE"
150  GOSUB 1000: REM  TRANSFORM CIRCLE
160  PRINT "X   Y   TRANSFORMED"
170  PRINT "------------------"
180  PRINT
190  FOR I = 1 TO NP
200  PRINT X2(I);"   ";Y2(I)
210  NEXT I
215  PRINT
216  PRINT "READY TO PLOT"
220  GOSUB 2000: REM  PLOT SHAPE
230  INPUT "ENTER Y TO REPLOT-";A$
240  IF A$ = "Y" GOTO 220
250  GOSUB 3000: REM  FIND V,P,F
260  INPUT "TYPE Y TO RECALCULATE V- ";A
270  IF A$ = "Y" GOTO 250
300  STOP
1000  REM  TRANSFORMS CIRCLE
1010  FOR I = 1 TO NP
1020 T1 = (I - 1) * 6.2832 / NP
1030 X1 = RC *  COS (T1) + XC
1040 Y1 = RC *  SIN (T1) + YC
1050 R1 =  SQR (X1 ^ 2 + Y1 ^ 2)
1060 SN = Y1 / R1:CS = X1 / R1
1070 X2(I) = (R1 + 1 / R1) * CS
1080 Y2(I) = (R1 - 1 / R1) * SN
1090  NEXT I
1100  RETURN
2000  REM  PLOTS TRANSFORMED CIRCLE
2010  INPUT "SCALE FACTOR? ";SF
2020  INPUT "X SHIFT? ";XS
2030  INPUT "Y SHIFT? ";YS
2040  HOME : VTAB 24
2050  HGR : HCOLOR= 3
2060  FOR I = 1 TO NP
```

```
2070 X1 = X2(I) * SF + XS
2080 Y1 = YS - Y2(I) * SF
2090  IF I = 1 GOTO 2200
2100  HPLOT  TO X1,Y1
2110  GOTO 2210
2200  HPLOT X1,Y1
2210  NEXT I
2220 X1 = X2(1) * SF + XS
2230 Y1 = YS - Y2(1) * SF
2240  HPLOT  TO X1,Y1
2250  RETURN
3000  REM  VEL. ON SURFACE
3010  INPUT "ANGLE OF FLOW? ";AF
3020  INPUT "CIRCULATION G/2PI? ";GC
3025  PRINT "FINDING VELOCITIES"
3026  TEXT
3030  FOR I = 1 TO NP
3040 T1 = 6.2832 * (I - 1) / NP
3050 P2(I) =  - 2 *  COS (T1 + AF) * RC + GC * T1
3060  NEXT I
3066 X2(NP + 1) = X2(1):Y2(NP + 1) = Y2(1)
3067 P2(NP + 1) = P2(1) + 6.2832 * GC
3070  FOR I = 1 TO NP
3080 DX = X2(I + 1) - X2(I)
3090 DY = Y2(I + 1) - Y2(I)
3100 DS =  SQR (DX ^ 2 + DY ^ 2)
3110 V2(I) = (P2(I + 1) - P2(I)) / DS
3200  NEXT I
3220  PRINT
3250  PRINT
3260  PRINT "VELOCITIES ON SURFACE"
3270  FOR I = 1 TO NP
3280  PRINT V2(I)
3290  NEXT I
3300  RETURN
```

```
RADIUS? 1.25
X CENTRE? .2
Y CENTRE? 0
NO. OF POINTS? 20
TRANSFORMING CIRCLE
X   Y   TRANSFORMED
-------------------

2.13965517  0
2.05715605  .200388149
1.81479049  .368649295
1.4276282  .478011277
.919941842  .512204264
```

```
.324797678   .469967905
-.314921405  .36780538
-.943367827  .238484817
-1.48847296  .121426882
-1.86624014  .0435185579
-2.00238095  -8.53791837E-07
-1.86622766  -.0435212157
-1.48845071  -.121431546
-.943339755  -.238490872
-.314891246  -.367811098
.324826937   -.469971482
.919967929   -.512204512
1.42764936   -.478007846
1.81480537   -.368642628
2.05716372   -.200379289

READY TO PLOT
SCALE FACTOR? 20
X SHIFT? 100
Y SHIFT? 70
ENTER Y TO REPLOT-N
ANGLE OF FLOW? 0
CIRCULATION G/2PI? 0
FINDING VELOCITIES

VELOCITIES ON SURFACE
.564632461
1.20353742
1.37475916
1.36964064
1.29482332
1.1925186
1.08619888
.992010107
.92061046
.856053799
-.856060301
-.92061321
-.992014031
-1.08620367
-1.19252363
-1.29482769
-1.36964297
-1.37475658
-1.20352174
-.564609027
TYPE Y TO RECALCULATE V- N
```

Program notes

(1) The dimension statement in line 100 sets up arrays for up to 100 points on the transformed shape. The x and y coordinates are stored in X2(100) and Y2(100), the velocity potential in P2(100) and the velocity in V2(100).
(2) Lines 110 to 140 input data on the circle to be transformed. The radius, RC, x and y-coordinates of the centre, XC, YC, and the number of points on the surface, NP, are called for.
(3) At line 145 a message to indicate that the program is continuing is printed.
(4) At line 150 the transformation subroutine is called and after this, in lines 160 to 210, the x, y coordinates of points on the new shape are printed.
(5) In lines 215 to 240 the subroutine to plot the new shape on the VDU is called and an option to change the plot provided.
(6) At line 250 the subroutine to calculate velocities on the new shape is called, an option to recalculate velocities is given and the program stops at line 300.
(7) Subroutine 1000 transforms the circle to a new shape by finding x, y coordinates for NP points from lines 1010 to 1090. The x, y coordinates of each point on the circle are found in lines 1020 to 1040. These are then transformed to new x, y values in lines 1050 to 1080. At line 1100 the routine returns to line 160.
(8) Subroutine 2000 plots the new shape. Scale factor SF, x-offset XS and y-offset YS are input in lines 2010 to 2030. Lines 2040 to 2050 set up the screen for plotting. In lines 2060 to 2240 the points are plotted. Each x and y value is scaled and offset to fit in the 360 × 160 picture space, in lines 2070 to 2080. The first point is selected by line 2090 and plotted as a single dot in line 2200. Other

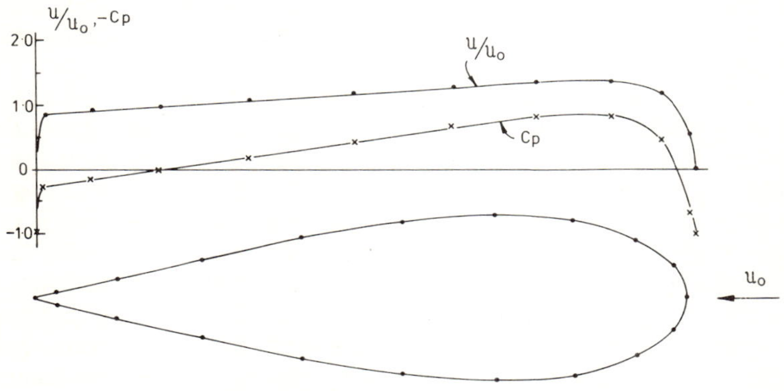

Figure 2.19 Velocities and pressures on a wing shape

points are joined by lines from the last point in lines 2100 and 2110. Finally, in lines 2220 to 2240 the last point is joined by a line to the first. In line 2250 the program returns to line 230.
(9) Subroutine 3000 calculates velocities. The angle of flow and circulation (AF and GC) are input in lines 3010 and 3025 and the screen reset for printing the velocities in 3026. From 3030 to 3060 the velocity potential P2(I) at each surface point is found. An extra point is set up in lines 3066 and 3067 so that the same calculation can be used for velocity at all points. In lines 3070 to 3200 this is used to find velocities from the gradient of P2 along the surface. Lines 3220 to 3290 print the velocity midway between the x, y points on the new shape. The program then returns to line 260.

Example 2.4 TRANC2: forces on a transformed circle

The forces on a circle in a steady flow were earlier shown to depend on the circulation round the body. This can be examined for other shapes by adapting the program TRANC1 so that it calculates pressures and forces on the shapes produced.

These matters can be explored by modifying the program TRANC1 to include the calculation of pressure coefficient, and the force coefficients described above. This has been done by adding to the subroutine 3000, as shown below. The program is now called TRANC2. The quantity CP(I), the pressure coefficient, has been stored instead of V2(I) since it is used to calculate CD and CL. In the same loop the elements of pressure force are added to CD and CL and the width and length of the body are found by adding the positive increases DX, DY, for each element of the surface, to the totals XT, YT.

The forces on an ellipse can be found by transforming the circle with radius 2.0 centred at (0,0). This gives an ellipse with major axis 5 and minor axis 3.

With angle of flow and circulation 0, CD and CL are zero. Recalculating with circulation $\Gamma/2\pi = 1$ produces a lift. The table following the listing summarizes some results for various shapes. The results for CD are not always accurate, with the shapes having a sharp edge caused by the original circle passing near (−1,0) or (+1,0). When the values of $\Gamma/2\pi$ and AF are chosen so that the velocity is small in this edge region then the solutions are more accurate. In fact this suggests the condition for the correct circulation about such a wing shape, called the Kutta condition, that the velocity should be zero at the sharp edge so that the flow leaves the edge smoothly rather than ‘turning a sharp corner’.

The drag coefficient C_D and lift coefficient C_L are calculated from the forces in the *x* and *y* directions by this program. Strictly speaking, these should be along and across the direction of the stream if we are to compare the results with potential flow formulae. Further lines can be incorporated to do this; for example

$$\begin{aligned}&CX = CD\\&CY = CL\\&CD = CX \times \cos(AF) + CY \times \sin(AF)\\&CL = -CX \times \sin(AF) + CY \times \cos(AF)\end{aligned}$$

```
3000  REM  V,P,F ON SHAPE
3010  INPUT "ANGLE OF FLOW? ";AF
3020  INPUT "CIRCULATION G/2PI? ";GC
3025  PRINT "FINDING FORCES"
3026  TEXT
3030  FOR I = 1 TO NP
3040 T1 = 6.2832 * (I - 1) / NP
3050 P2(I) =  - 2 *  COS (T1 + AF) * RC + GC * T1
3060  NEXT I
3065 CD = 0:CL = 0:XT = 0:YT = 0
3066 X2(NP + 1) = X2(1):Y2(NP + 1) = Y2(1)
3067 P2(NP + 1) = P2(1) + 6.2832 * GC
3070  FOR I = 1 TO NP
3080 DX = X2(I + 1) - X2(I)
3090 DY = Y2(I + 1) - Y2(I)
3100 DS =  SQR (DX ^ 2 + DY ^ 2)
3110 V2 = (P2(I + 1) - P2(I)) / DS
3120 CP(I) = 1 - V2 ^ 2
3130 CD = CD + CP(I) * DY
3140 CL = CL + CP(I) * DX
3150  IF DX < 0 GOTO 3180
3160 XT = XT + DX
3180  IF DY < 0 GOTO 3200
3190 YT = YT + DY
3200  NEXT I
3210 CD = CD / YT:CL = CL / XT
3220  PRINT
3230  PRINT "DRAG COEFF.= ";CD
3240  PRINT "LIFT COEFF.= ";CL
3300  RETURN
```

```
]RUN
RADIUS? 2
X CENTRE? 0
Y CENTRE? 0
NO. OF POINTS? 20
TRANSFORMING CIRCLE
X   Y   TRANSFORMED
-------------------

2.5  0
2.37764072  .46352654
2.02254033  .881679662
1.46945867  1.21352744
.772535499  1.42658614
-9.18346824E-06  1.5
-.772552967  1.42658273
-1.46947354  1.21352096
-2.02255112  .881670746
-2.3776464  .463516059
-2.5  -1.10201619E-05
-2.37763505  -.46353702
-2.02252953  -.881688577
-1.46944381  -1.21353391
-.772518024  -1.42658954
2.7554062E-05  -1.5
.772570442  -1.42657933
1.46948839  -1.21351448
2.02256192  -.881661831
2.37765208  -.463505574

READY TO PLOT
SCALE FACTOR? 30
X SHIFT? 120
Y SHIFT? 80
ENTER Y TO REPLOT-N
ANGLE OF FLOW? 0
CIRCULATION G/2PI? 1
FINDING FORCES

DRAG COEFF.= -3.25889308E-06
LIFT COEFF.= 2.51328095
TYPE Y TO RECALCULATE- N
```

Results: TRANC2

R_C (m)	X_C (m)	Y_C (m)	AF (rad)	$\Gamma/2\pi$ (m^2/s)	CX	CY	XT (m)	YT (m)
2	0	0	0	0	0	0	5	3
2	0	0	0	1.0	0	2.51	5	3
2	0	0	$\pi/2$	1.0	−4.188	0	5	3
2	0	0	0	2.0	1.8E−5	5.02	5	3
1.25	0.25	0.25	0	0	−0.1109	0.1584	4.13	1.29
1.25	0.25	0.25	$\pi/20$	0	−0/47	−0.4915	4.13	1.29
1.25	0.25	0	0	0	3E−4	4E−7	4.17	1.07
1.25	0.25	0	$\pi/20$	0	−0.14	−1.3E−3	4.17	1.07
1.25	0.25	0	$\pi/20$	1	−2.18	2.98	4.17	1.07
1.25	0.25	0	$\pi/20$	0.4	−0.07	1.008	4.17	1.07
1.0	0	0	0	0	4E−9	2E−10	4.0	4E−9
1.0	0	0	0	1	−0.517	3.1416	4.0	4E−9
			$\pi/2$	+0	0.336	2E−6	4.0	4E−9

Program notes

(1) The main part of the program is the same as TRANC1 except for an array CP(100) to hold pressure coefficients. The subroutine contains the major changes.
(2) In subroutine 3000 the pressure coefficients and force coefficients are calculated from the velocities and the force coefficient printed. Lines 3010 to 3020 input the angle of flow and circulation as in TRANC1. In line 3025 a message 'FINDING FORCES' is printed, and the screen cleared for printing further results by line 3026.
(3) Lines 3030 to 3060 find the velocity potential at points on the transformed shape. Line 3065 sets initial values for the integration which will calculate force coefficients CD (drag) and CL (lift). XT and YT will be the length and width of the new shape.
(4) In the loop from line 3070 to 3200 velocities are calculated from potential gradients between each pair of points on the new shape (line 3080 to 3110). The pressure coefficients CP(**I**) are found from these velocities at line 3120. Lines 3130 and 3140 add the contribution of each element of surface to the force coefficients. Lines 3150 to 3190 add the contributions of each surface element to the length and width of the shape if these increments are positive.
(5) Line 3210 completes the calculation of the force coefficients. The results are printed in lines 3230 and 3240.

Example 2.5 FDBL: boundary layer on a flat plate

The calculation of velocities in a laminar boundary layer on a flat plate can be made according to the scheme of Section 2.12. A program to implement this is given below. The first line, 100, sets up matrices to store the *y*-coordinates and velocities of points in the boundary layer. In lines 110 to 160 the data to control the calculation are input. Lines 180 to 210 calculate some preliminary quantities, such as the initial velocity profile ($U = 1.0$ at all points across the layer). Lines 220 to 450 then calculate and print the velocity profiles required. The loop from lines 250 to 320 computes the velocity one step downstream for each point across the layer. The *y*-coordinates are also found. This is then done for J2 steps (by the loop from line 230 to 330) between each printing of the velocity profile. Velocity profiles are printed in lines 310 to 420. A typical set of inputs and results is given after the program. These are plotted in Figure 2.18 in a form suitable for comparison with the exact solution due to Blasius.

Program FDBL

```
100  DIM Y(20),U(2,20)
110  INPUT "NO. STEPS ACROSS FLOW? ";K2
120  INPUT "NO. PROFILES? ";P2
130  INPUT "NO. STEPS BETWEEN PROFILES? ";J2
140  INPUT "VISCOSITY? ";NU
150  INPUT "S STEP? ";DS
160  INPUT "X STEP? ";DX
170  PRINT "CALCULATING PROFILE"
180 D1 = DX * NU / (2 * DS ^ 2)
190  FOR K = 2 TO K2
200 U(1,K) = 1
210  NEXT K
220  FOR P = 1 TO P2
230  FOR J = 1 TO J2
240 U(1,1) = 0:U(1,K2) = 1
250  FOR K = 2 TO K2 - 1
260 D2 = U(1,K + 1) ^ 2 + U(1,K - 1) ^ 2 - 2 * U(1,K) ^ 2
270 U(2,K) = U(1,K) + D1 * D2
280 Y(K) = Y(K - 1) + 2 * DS / (U(2,K) + U(2,K - 1))
290  NEXT K
300  FOR K = 2 TO K2 - 1
310 U(1,K) = U(2,K)
320  NEXT K
330  NEXT J
340  PRINT
350 X1 = P * J2 * DX
360  PRINT "VELOCITY PROFILE AT X              =";X1;" M"
```

```
370  PRINT
380  PRINT "Y M ","U M/S "
390  PRINT "----","------"
400  FOR K = 1 TO K2
410  PRINT Y(K),U(1,K)
420  NEXT K
450  NEXT P
500  STOP


]RUN
NO. STEPS ACROSS FLOW? 10
NO. PROFILES? 3
NO. STEPS BETWEEN PROFILES? 10
VISCOSITY? 1E-6
S STEP? 2.5E-4
X STEP? 1E-2
CALCULATING PROFILE

VELOCITY PROFILE AT X              =.1 M

Y M               U M/S
----              ------
0                 0
7.41658328E-04    .674164883
1.06591284E-03    .867833689
1.34041841E-03    .953623023
1.59809367E-03    .98680382
1.85012397E-03    .997084649
2.10054946E-03    .999517216
2.35061703E-03    .999942347
2.60062482E-03    .999995324
0                 1

VELOCITY PROFILE AT X              =.2 M

Y M               U M/S
----              ------
0                 0
8.55520118E-04    .584439792
1.22235766E-03    .778561385
1.52252781E-03    .887160547
1.79513119E-03    .94700601
2.05493051E-03    .977556383
2.30885116E-03    .99156267
2.56026089E-03    .997222729
2.81070356E-03    .999242215
0                 1

VELOCITY PROFILE AT X              =.3 M
```

```
Y M               U M/S
----              ------
0                 0
9.35826986E-04    .534286794
1.33374947E-03    .722239343
1.65444043E-03    .83689409
1.94092732E-03    .908386479
2.20975501E-03    .951540956
2.46913117E-03    .976161252
2.72352302E-03    .989310583
2.9753656E-03     .996056568
0                 1
```

Program notes

(1) Line 100 dimensions arrays Y(20) and U(20,2) to contain the y-coordinates and velocity in the x-direction of up to 20 points across the boundary layer.
(2) Lines 110 to 160 input the data. These are: K2, the number of steps across the layer; the number of profiles, P2; and J2, the number of steps in the x-direction between outputs of the velocity profile. Also the kinematic viscosity NU, the step in stream function DS, and the step in x, DX are input.
(3) At 170 a message is printed: 'CALCULATING PROFILE'. This shows that no further data is required and the program is proceeding.
(4) At line 180 the constant $\Delta x\nu/2\Delta\psi^2$ is found. Then the initial velocity profile $U = 1.0$ is set up right across the layer in lines 190 to 210.
(5) The loop from 220 to 450 finds and prints the required number of profiles. Within this loop is the loop from line 230 to 330 which marches downstream by J2 steps of Δx. For each downstream step the loop from 250 to 320 calculates the velocity at each of K2 points across the boundary layer.
(6) At line 240 the velocity is set to zero on the inner edge and 1.0 on the outer edge of the layer. In the loop from 250 to 290 U(2,K) at downstream points are calculated from U(1,K) at upstream points. The y-coordinates of these downstream points are also found.
(7) In the loop from 300 to 320 the downstream velocities become the upstream values for the next step.
(8) In lines 340 to 410 the y and U values in the velocity profile are printed. The program ends at line 500.

PROBLEMS

(**2.1**) Find the stream function ψ and velocity potential ϕ for a potential flow vortex, by writing a program similar to Example 2.1. Check that the flow is incompressible and irrotational by finding ψ and ϕ in the neighbourhood of a small square of fluid and showing that the values satisfy a form of Laplace's equation.
(**2.2**) Plot the streamlines for a source of flow $q = 8\,\text{m}^2/\text{s}$ in a uniform stream of velocity $U = 0.5\,\text{m/s}$. Check that this represents the flow round a half-body whose surface is given by the equation

$$r = q\theta/2\pi U \sin\theta$$

(**2.3**) Find the length and height of a mound which is represented by a source and sink of flow $10\,\text{m}^2/\text{s}$ placed 2 m apart in a stream of velocity 25 m/s.
(**2.4**) Write a program to calculate the position of streamlines in a flow past a circular cylinder. This can be done on a grid system as in Example 2.2 or by using the equation

$$\sin\theta = \frac{\psi}{U_0\left(r - \dfrac{a^2}{r}\right)}$$

Calculate also the pressure on the surface of the cylinder and the forces in line and across the stream. Find the minimum pressure and the force on a pipe of diameter 0.5 m lying half buried in a flat bed with a current of velocity 0.75 m/s ($\rho = 1000\,\text{kg/m}^3$).
(**2.5**) Investigate, using the program TRANC1 or TRANC2, the values of circulation Γ which enable the flow to leave a sharp trailing edge smoothly. The shape used could be a flat plate. The value of Γ required to give zero tangential velocity at the trailing edge should be

$$\Gamma = \pi C\, U_0 \sin AF$$

where AF = angle of flow to the plate
C = width of plate
(**2.6**) When a stream is accelerated past a body, or a body is accelerated in a still fluid, there will be inertia forces on the body. These are a result of the $\partial\phi/\partial t$ terms in Bernoulli's equation. These can be included in the force calculation of the program TRANC2. For example, the velocity potential at a point 1 on the body is proportional to the stream velocity, i.e. $\phi_1 = K_1 U_0$ so $\partial\phi_1/\partial t = K_1 (\partial U_0/\partial t)$. Using the unsteady part of the Bernoulli equation, since

in many problems we can ignore the other terms, the pressure at point 1 is

$$p_1 = p_0 + \rho \frac{\partial \phi_0}{\partial t} - \rho \frac{\partial \phi_1}{\partial t}$$

We can integrate the inertia pressures for all points on the body surface in the same way as Example 2.3, to find the forces due to inertia effects, $F_x I$ and $F_y I$. These are conveniently expressed as inertia coefficients

$$C_{Mx} = \frac{F_x I}{\rho \pi D^2 \dfrac{\partial U_0}{\partial t}}$$

where D = width of body.

Using the program TRANC2 with suitable modifications, find the inertia coefficients for a flat plate and an ellipse with major to minor axis ratio of 2 to 1.

(2.7) Test the effect of varying the quantity $\mu \Delta x / 2\rho \Delta\psi^2$ in the boundary layer calculation by changing the quantities Δx, $\Delta\psi$ etc. The values in the example were arrived at by estimating the boundary layer thickness at the x distance where results were required from Blasius' expression. Then about 10 points were fitted in this thickness assuming ψ is very approximately $U_0 y$. The distance Δx was then estimated from the assumption that $\mu \Delta x / 2\rho \Delta\psi^2$ should be less than 1/2, which would apply to the diffusion equation of similar (though linear) form. The value of Δx was adjusted after one trial calculation which appeared unstable and $\mu \Delta x / 2\rho \Delta\psi^2 = 1/12.5$ was finally used. If different values of fluid viscosity μ or density ρ are used then Δx and $\Delta\psi$ must be adjusted. Try a calculation with a more viscous fluid. The calculation could be made stable for any values of Δx, $\Delta\psi$, etc. by using velocities halfway along the Δx step instead of at the beginning. This would be an implicit as opposed to an explicit calculation scheme and require some iteration as the velocities $U_{J+1/2,k} = (U_{J,K} + U_{J+K})/2$ etc. are not known at the start of the step. However, this could be built into the program quite readily.

(2.8) The effect of a pressure gradient on the boundary layer calculated can be tested by including the term $(-\mathrm{d}p/\mathrm{d}x)(1/\rho U_{J,K})$. Using Bernoulli's equation, the pressure gradient can be found from the velocity at the outer edge of the layer as $-\rho U_e(\mathrm{d}U_e/\mathrm{d}x)$. This variable edge velocity U_e must be included in the program. A possible variation for U_e would be that given by a source placed a distance a in front of a flat plate, $U_e = q/(2x + a)$. Another variation that could be tried is the potential flow velocity at the surface of a circular cylinder, $U_e = 2U_0 \sin\theta$. In this case the boundary layer must be given some initial non-zero profile, for example by starting with uniform velocity at $\theta = \theta_1$. Then $x = a(\theta - \theta_1)$, where a = radius of circle.

Chapter 3

Numerical solutions to potential flows

ESSENTIAL THEORY

3.1 General approach

The analytical solutions to potential flow are limited in number and may not happen to fit the particular problem we have in mind. A solution of Laplace's equation is found but then the physical situation represented by the solution has to be identified. We would prefer to set up the conditions representing a particular problem and then obtain the solution for the flow. This will usually involve an approximate numerical method in which a computer is essential to solve the large number of equations generated. Whatever the details of the method it will require input of some geometrical details to define the boundaries and possibly also to divide the region inside the boundaries into sections. The value of the potential function or its gradient must be specified on the boundary as well. The computer program will then calculate values of the potential function and these must be used to provide the information required by the user; for example, velocities, pressures, etc. Three such numerical methods are described briefly in the following sections: the finite difference (FDM), finite element (FEM) and boundary element (BEM) methods.

3.2 The finite difference method—principles

The basis of this method is to represent the continuous variation of the potential function by a set of values at points on a grid of intersecting lines; see Figure 3.1. The gradients of the function are then represented by differences in the values at neighbouring points and a finite difference version of the equation of potential flow is formed. At points in the interior of the grid this equation is used to form a set of simultaneous equations giving the value of the potential function at a point in terms of values at nearby points. At the edges of the grid the value of the function is fixed, or a special form of the finite difference equation is used, to give the required gradient of the function.

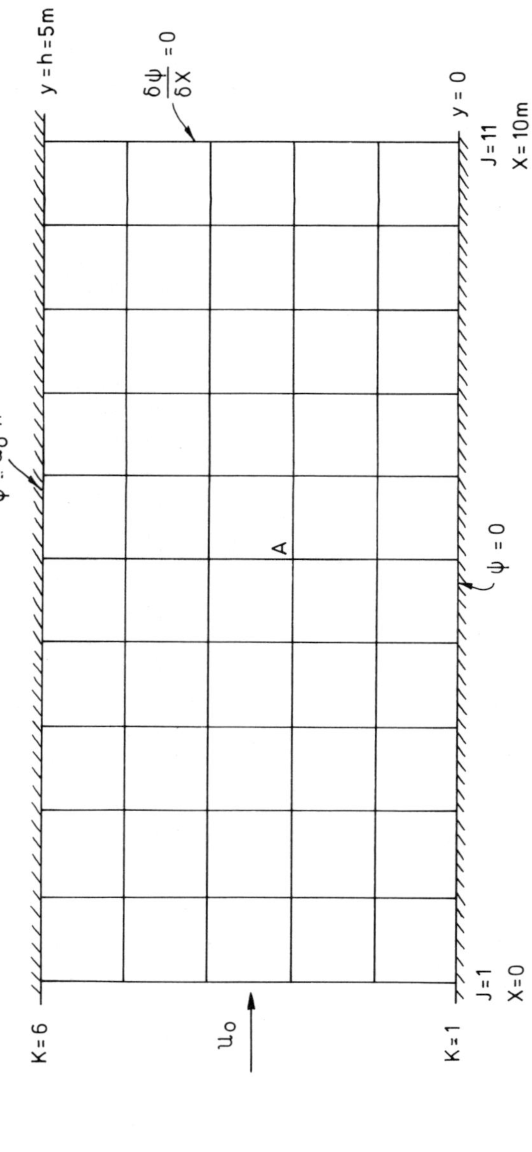

Figure 3.1 Finite difference grid for a simple flow

3.3 Finite difference equations

In a regular rectangular grid the finite difference form of Laplace's equation is particularly simple. If we denote a grid point by the suffixes J,K and consider the surrounding points, as sketched below, then we find the following approximations to the gradients of a potential function

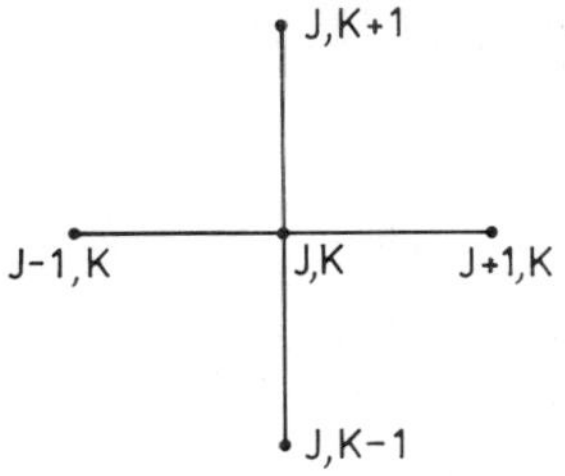

$$\frac{\partial \phi_{J+1/2,K}}{\partial x} \simeq \frac{\phi_{J+1,K} - \phi_{J,K}}{\Delta x}$$

$$\frac{\partial^2 \phi_{J,K}}{\partial x^2} \simeq \frac{\dfrac{\phi_{J+1,K} - \phi_{J,K}}{\Delta x} - \dfrac{\phi_{J,K} - \phi_{J-1,K}}{\Delta x}}{\Delta x}$$

$$= \frac{\phi_{J+1,K} + \phi_{J-1,K} - 2\phi_{J,K}}{\Delta x^2}$$

so

$$\frac{\partial^2 \phi_{J,K}}{\partial x^2} + \frac{\partial^2 \phi_{J,K}}{\partial y^2} \simeq \frac{\phi_{J+1,K} + \phi_{J-1,K} - 2\phi_{J,K}}{\Delta x^2} + \frac{\phi_{J-K+1} + \phi_{J,K-1} - 2\phi_{J,K}}{\Delta y^2}$$

so if: $(\partial^2\phi/\partial x^2) + (\partial^2\phi/\partial y^2) = 0$ and $\Delta x = \Delta y$

$$\phi_{J+1,K} + \phi_{J-1,K} + \phi_{J,K-1} + \phi_{J,K-1} - 4\phi_{J,K} = 0$$

$$\phi_{J,K} = (\phi_{J+1,K} + \phi_{J-1,K} + \phi_{J,K+1} + \phi_{J,K-1})/4 \qquad (3.1)$$

It is interesting to note that the same equation applies in a grid having the properties of the flow net; that is, formed of curvilinear squares. A direct formulation of the continuity equation at a grid point gives, for the velocity potential

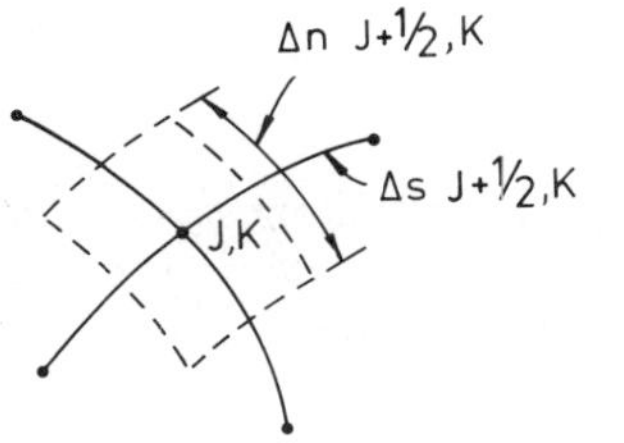

$$+ (\phi_{J,K+1} - \phi_{J,K}) \left.\frac{\Delta s}{\Delta n}\right|_{J,K+1/2}$$

$$- (\phi_{J,K} - \phi_{J,K-1}) \left.\frac{\Delta s}{\Delta n}\right|_{J,K-1/2}$$

$$+ (\phi_{J+1,K} - \phi_{J,K}) \left.\frac{\Delta n}{\Delta s}\right|_{J+1/2,K}$$

$$- (\phi_{J,K} - \phi_{J-1,K}) \left.\frac{\Delta n}{\Delta s}\right|_{J-1/2,K}$$

$$= 0$$

In the grid of curvilinear squares, $\Delta s = \Delta n$ so we get back to Equation 3.1.

3.4 Finite differences – boundary values

A good number of flows can be represented by fixed values of the potential function on the boundaries. This simply requires the edge points in the grid to be omitted from the calculation once the appropriate boundary value has been assigned to them.

This can be done by including an array in the computer program which indicates for each point whether the finite difference equation is to be used at that point or not. Another possibility for some flows is to store the width of the flow at each column of the grid and only work with these points in this width.

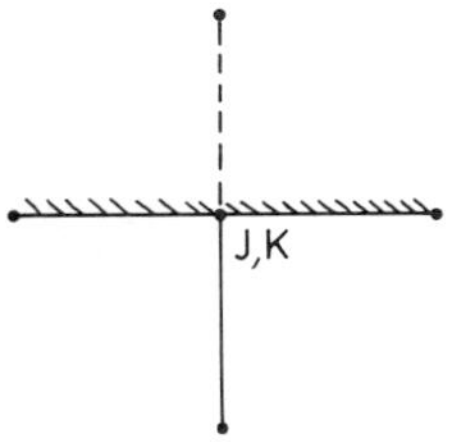

Many flows require a fixed value of the gradient of the function on part of the boundary. This results in a special form of the finite difference equation for boundary points. For example, points on the top line of a grid representing a horizontal wall will have the condition $\partial\phi/\partial y = 0$. The point J,K+1 does not now exist, but if it did and if $\phi_{J,K+1} = \phi_{J,K-1}$ then the boundary condition would be ensured. We can produce this effect by using the equation

$$\phi_{J,K} = (\phi_{J+1,K} + \phi_{J-1,K} + 2\phi_{J,K-1})/4 \qquad (3.2)$$

3.5 Solution of finite difference equations

A convenient method of solving the finite difference equations is that of successive over-relaxation (SOR). In relaxation, Equation 3.1 is applied at each internal grid point in turn and the process repeated until the correct solution is obtained. This is indicated by the change in $\phi_{J,K}$ between one iteration and the next at any point becoming small; more directly, by the residual

$$R = \phi_{J,K+1} + \phi_{J,K-1} + \phi_{J+1,K} + \phi_{J-1,K} - 4\phi_{J,K}$$

becoming nearly zero. The number of iterations can be reduced by over-relaxation adding more than the change in ϕ to the previous value. That is,

$$\phi^{n+1}_{J,K} = \phi^{n}_{J,K} + \text{ORF}\,(\phi^{n+1}_{J,K} - \phi^{n}_{J,K})$$

where $\phi^{n}_{J,K}$ = ϕ value after n iterations
ORF = over-relaxation factor.

A value of ORF of between 1 and 2 is used; generally, 1.8 is a suitable value.

3.6 The finite element method

This method allows the region filled with fluid to be divided up in a much more flexible way than was possible with the finite difference method. The nodes at which the value of the potential function is found do not have to lie on a grid system but can be on a flexible mesh; see, for example, Figure 3.2. The boundary conditions are also handled in a more convenient manner so that a standard program can deal very easily with most conditions. The result is a

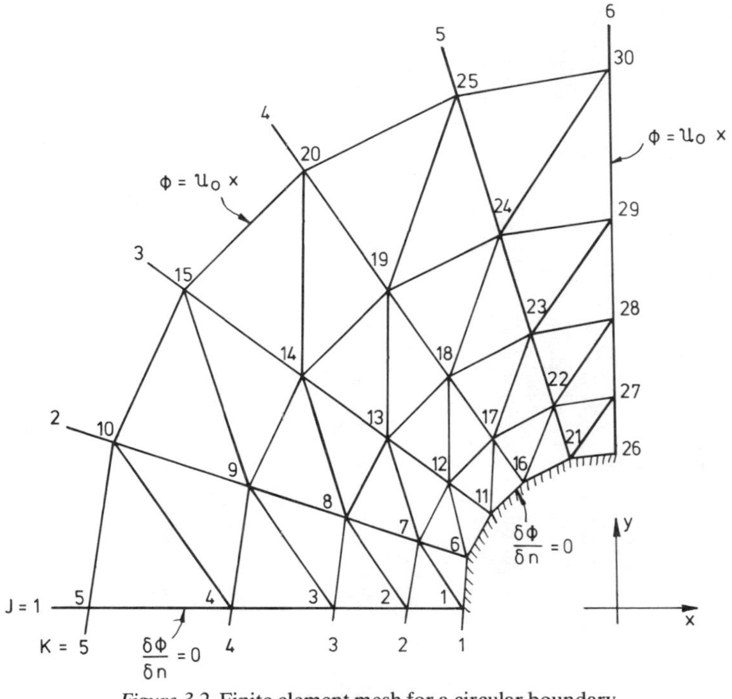

Figure 3.2 Finite element mesh for a circular boundary

program which can calculate flows for many shapes and types of boundary.

The freedom from a grid system is gained by the underlying principles of the method. This can be one of a number of principles classed as variational or as weighted residual methods. The briefest explanation for potential flows is provided by a variational principle. One possible principle is that the solution must be one in which the energy of the flow is a minimum. For incompressible flow, strain energy cannot be stored so we find a flow with minimum kinetic energy (this being the only part of the total energy which can change). In terms of velocity potential ϕ kinetic energy is

$$\mathrm{KE} = \frac{\rho}{2}\int_A \int \left[\left(\frac{\partial \phi}{\partial x}\right)^2 + \left(\frac{\partial \phi}{\partial y}\right)^2\right] \mathrm{d}x\mathrm{d}y \tag{3.3}$$

Thus n equations can be found for n unknown ϕ values by requiring that

$$\frac{\partial(\mathrm{KE})}{\partial \phi_i} = 0, \quad i = 1 \text{ to } n$$

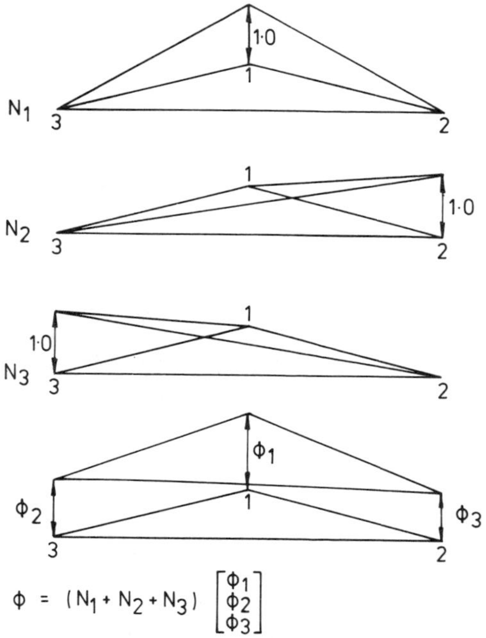

Figure 3.3 Finite element shape functions

In order to express the integrals in terms of the ϕ_i values we divide the flow region into elements in which ϕ can be expressed as simple functions of position and the ϕ_i values at the corners or nodes of the element; see Figure 3.3.

The shape functions giving ϕ are written

$$\phi = [N_1, N_2, N_3] \begin{bmatrix} \phi_1 \\ \phi_2 \\ \phi_3 \end{bmatrix}$$

$$N_1 = (A^0{}_1 + b_1 x + a_1 y)/2A$$

$$N_2 = (A^0{}_2 + b_2 x + a_2 y)/2A$$

$$N_3 = (A^0{}_3 + b_3 x + a_3 y)/2A$$

where A = area of triangular element

$= b_1 a^0{}_2 - b_2 a_1$

$a_i = x_k - x_j,\ b_i = y_j - y_k$

$A_i^0 = x_j\, y_k - x_k\, y_j$

$i = 1,2,3,\ j = 2,3,1,\ k = 3,1,2$

And from these definitions

$$\frac{\partial \phi}{\partial x} = \left[\frac{\partial N_1}{\partial x}, \frac{\partial N_2}{\partial x}, \frac{\partial N_3}{\partial x}\right] \begin{bmatrix} \phi_1 \\ \phi_2 \\ \phi_3 \end{bmatrix}$$

$$= \frac{1}{2A} [b_1, b_2, b_3] \begin{bmatrix} \phi_1 \\ \phi_2 \\ \phi_3 \end{bmatrix}$$

The kinetic energy in an element will thus be

$$\mathrm{KE}|\, e = \rho/2 \iint \frac{1}{4A^2} [b_1\,\phi_1 + b_2\,\phi_2 + b_3\,\phi_3]^2 + \frac{1}{4A^2} [a_1\,\phi_1 + a_2\,\phi_2 + a_3\,\phi_3]^2 \mathrm{d}x\mathrm{d}y$$

$$= \rho/2 \left(\frac{1}{4A} [b_1\,\phi_1 + b_2\,\phi_2 + b_3\,\phi_3]^2 + \frac{1}{4A} [a_1\,\phi_1 + a_2\,\phi_2 + a_3\,\phi_3]^2 \right)$$

and

$$\frac{\partial KE}{\partial \phi_1}\Big| e = \rho/2 \frac{2}{4A} [b_1 \phi_1 + b_2 \phi_2 + b_3 \phi_3]\, b_1$$

$$+ \rho/2 \frac{2}{4A} [a_1 \phi_1 + a_2 \phi_2 + a_3 \phi_3] a_l$$

The contribution for an element to the equation for ϕ_i can thus be written

$$[Se]\,[\phi_i] = 0$$

with

$$Se_{ij} = \frac{1}{4A} (b_i\, b_j + a_i\, a_j) \qquad (3.4)$$

$$i = 1, 2, 3; j = 1, 2, 3$$

And the complete equations for ϕ are obtained by adding the contributions from all the element equations to give

$$[S]\,[\phi]$$

The terms in [S] are built up by a statement

$$\text{Add } Se_{ij} \text{ to } S_{NiNj} \qquad (3.5)$$

Where element node i is the node number Ni in the mesh.

A finite element program will take data on each of the elements (e.g. the node coordinates and numbers of the nodes in the overall system) and build up a matrix equation for ϕ in the way indicated. This equation can then be solved by a standard method.

The boundary conditions for a finite element calculation are dealt with in one of two ways. If the value of ϕ is specified on the boundary the matrix equation is modified, usually by making the diagonal term equal to 1 and all other terms zero for the node in question. The right-hand side is simply made equal to the specified value.

That is, if $\phi_k = C$ then we make $S_{kk} = 1$, $S_{kj} = 0$, $T_k = C$ in the system of equations

$$[S]\,[\phi] = [T] \qquad (3.6)$$

If the value of $\partial\phi/\partial n$ (normal gradient of ϕ, equal to velocity at right angles to boundary) is specified we include this by going back to the basic variational equation. The statement now is that the KE is minimized subject to the condition that $\partial\phi/\partial n = q$ on part of the boundary. This can be accomplished by minimizing the function

$$\mathrm{KE}_1 = \rho/2 \int_A \int \left(\frac{\partial\phi}{\partial x}\right)^2 + \left(\frac{\partial\phi}{\partial y}\right)^2 \mathrm{d}x\mathrm{d}y + \rho \int_B \phi . \frac{\partial\phi}{\partial n} \mathrm{d}s \quad (3.7)$$

where B = boundary of flow
S = direction along B.

Obviously, if $\partial\phi/\partial n = 0$ the equations are unchanged from their previous form. In this commonly found case we need not make any special arrangements in the program to produce a $\partial\phi/\partial n = 0$ boundary condition. It is called the natural boundary condition. It should be remembered that this is the condition at any nodes on the boundary which are not otherwise dealt with.

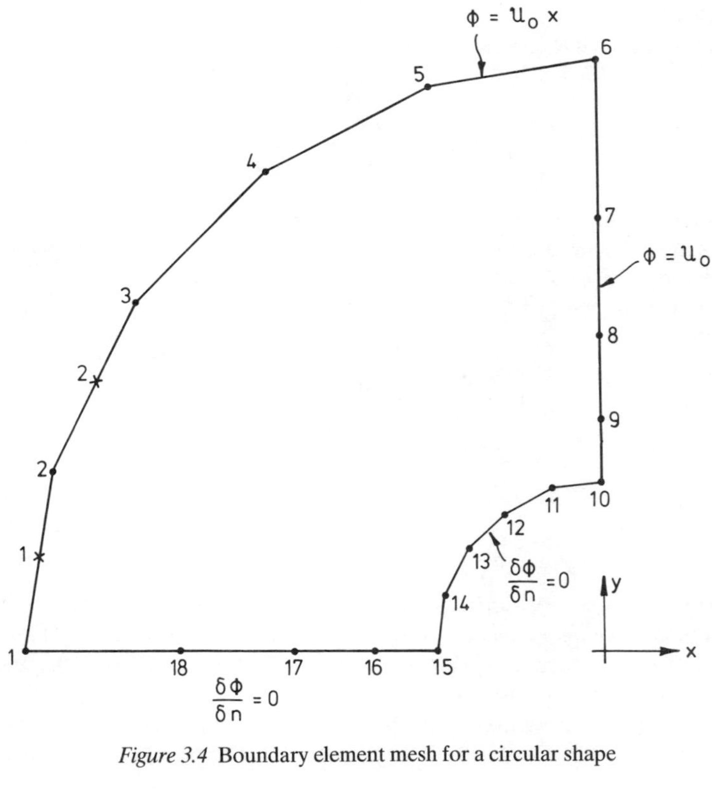

Figure 3.4 Boundary element mesh for a circular shape

3.7 Boundary element methods

The BEM is another method which adapts easily to any boundary shape. The advantage over the FEM is that the region containing the fluid need not be divided into elements. Calculations are only necessary at points on the boundary. For example, a BEM mesh for same problem as the FEM mesh is shown in Figure 3.4.

The method is based on Green's theorem, which allows the Laplace equation to be integrated over the fluid region A, so that only terms on the boundary, B, are required

$$\iint_A (\phi^*\nabla^2\phi - \phi\nabla^2\phi^*)\,\mathrm{d}A = \int_B \left(\phi^* \frac{\partial\phi}{\partial n} - \phi\frac{\partial\phi^*}{\partial n}\mathrm{d}s\right) \tag{3.8}$$

Now if we take a point i in the region A, and specify ϕ^* as the function which is a solution of

$$\nabla^2\phi^* = -\Delta i \text{ (where } \Delta i = \text{Dirac delta function)}$$

Then at point i, $\nabla^2\phi^* = 1$ and $\nabla^2\phi = 0$ (since ϕ is the function satisfying Laplace's equation which we want to find).

we have then, for ϕ_i

$$\phi_{\mathrm{i}} = \int\left(\phi^* \frac{\partial\phi}{\partial n} - \phi\frac{\partial\phi^*}{\partial n}\right)\mathrm{d}s \tag{3.9}$$

Suppose that the boundary is divided into M sections called boundary elements and the value of ϕ is given in each section; for example, take ϕ as constant in each section. Then applying Equation 3.9 at a point in each boundary element gives

$$\phi_i = \sum_{j=1}^{M}\int_{Bj}\left(\phi^*\frac{\partial\phi_j}{\partial n}\right)\mathrm{d}s - \sum_{j=1}^{M}\int_{Bj}\left(\phi_{\mathrm{j}}\frac{\partial\phi^*}{\partial n}\right)\mathrm{d}s$$

or

$$\phi_i + \sum_{j=1}^{M}\int_{Bj}\left(\phi_j\frac{\partial\phi^*}{\partial n}\right)ds = \sum_{j=1}^{M}\int_{Bj}\left(\phi^*\frac{\partial\phi_j}{\partial n}\right)\mathrm{d}s \tag{3.10}$$

If ϕ^* is known we can evaluate the coefficients in this equation, which involves ϕ at all the boundary elements. Assembling all the other similar equations for each element will give us a matrix equation which we can solve for ϕ.

ϕ need not be constant in an element, of course. If it varies linearly, for example, there will be two unknown ϕs in each element (but since the elements join end to end we could have the same number of unknowns as with constant ϕ). The equations like 3.10 would be written for the points at the end of each element. The boundary conditions for the problem can be in terms of ϕ values at some points and $\partial\phi/\partial n$ values at others, so that the matrix equation

$$[H]\{\phi\} = [G]\left\{\frac{\partial\phi}{\partial n}\right\} \tag{3.11}$$

may need to be rearranged before it is solved.

The solution of $\nabla^2\phi^* = \Delta i$, which we need to find the matrix coefficients, is, fortunately, well known and is just the flow due to a unit source (or sink). The expressions are

$$\begin{aligned}\phi^* &= \frac{1}{2\pi}\ln r \\ \frac{\partial\phi^*}{\partial r} &= \frac{1}{2\pi r}\end{aligned} \tag{3.12}$$

3.8 Bibliography

1. Brebbia, C. A. (Ed), *Recent advances in the boundary element method*, Pentech Press (1980).
2. Brebbia, C. A., *The boundary element method for engineers*, Pentech Press (1978).
3. Brebbia, C. A. and Connor, J. J., *Finite element techniques for fluid flow*, Newnes Butterworth (1976).
4. Zienkiewicz, O. C., *The finite element method in engineering science*, 2nd Edition, McGraw-Hill (1971).
5. Mitchell, A. R. and Griffiths, D. F., *Finite differences*, Wiley (1980).

WORKED EXAMPLES

Example 3.1 FDIT1: finite difference solution for flow through a channel

The stream function ψ is chosen as the calculation variable and in this simple problem the boundary conditions are as shown in Figure 3.1. The flow region is a rectangle with no flow through the top and bottom sides and flow parallel to the x-direction at the inflow and outflow (on the left-hand and right-hand edges respectively). The dimensions of the rectangle are 10 m long by 5 m wide with a flow of 5 m^3/s between the walls per unit depth of flow. We can thus fit a regular grid of 11 lines by 6 lines to the fluid region. On the bottom row of points ψ will be constant with a value we can set equal to zero. On the top row $\psi = 5\,m^2/s$ and at the ends of the channel $\partial\phi/\partial x = 0$. The ψ values on the internal points are found by the successive over-relaxation method. A program to do this is shown below.

In line 100 the array S to store the stream function ψ is set up, together with an array W to store vorticity if needed in later versions of the program (this will not be used in the present example).

Lines 110 to 116 read in the data and set the boundary conditions for constant ψ values. M1 is the number of iterations in the SOR process, and R1 the over-relaxation factor. J2 is the number of columns in the finite difference grid and K2 the number of rows. H1, read at line 112, is the height of the channel from which the stream function value on the top wall is calculated, assuming a unit inflow velocity. This value is then assigned to the top row of grid points in lines 114 to 116. The bottom row is assumed to have $\psi = 0$ so no statements are needed to achieve this. Lines 180 and 190 calculate variables R2 = 1−R1 and R3 = R1/4 to save repeated calculations of these quantities in the iteration loop. This is the next stage of the program, from lines 200 to 310. The end grid columns are dealt with in lines 220 to 223, making the horizontal gradient of ψ zero by setting ψ values equal to their values at the immediate upstream or downstream points. The main block of internal grid points is then dealt with by the standard finite difference version of the Laplace equation in lines 250 to 300. The grid is worked through column by column from left to right and bottom to top of each column.

In lines 270 to 271, S4 the sum of the ψ values at the four surrounding points is found. In line 275 the circulation W(J,K) at the central point is added to S4 (W(J,K) = 0 in this case). Line 280 calculates the latest value of ψ at point J,K from its previous value and S4.

After M1 iterations of this process the ψ values on a number of grid rows can be printed. This is done in lines 320 to 332. The lines selected for printing are read in line 322. The data appears in lines 400 to 420.

The result from three typical runs are shown after the program. The problem was chosen because the solution is easily seen to be $\psi = U_0 y = \mathrm{K}-1$. Thus the value calculated for grid row K = 3 should be $\psi = 2.0$. We see that in the first run, starting from an initial state of $\psi = 0$ for each internal point, M1 = 10 iterations with an over-relaxation factor of 1.0 does not produce an acceptable solution. The second run with M1 = 10 and R1 = 1.8 however gets close to correct solution and the third run with M1 = 20 and R1 = 1.8 is extremely close.

Program FDIT1

```
100 DIM S(21,21),W(21,21)
110 READ M1,R1,J2,K2
112 READ H1
114 FOR J=1 TO J2
115 S(J,K2)=H1
116 NEXT J
180 R2=1.0-R1
190 R3=R1/4
200 FOR M=1 TO M1
220 FOR K=1 TO K2
221 S(1,K)=S(2,K)
222 S(J2,K)=S(J2-1,K)
223 NEXT K
250 FOR J=2 TO J2-1
260 FOR K=2 TO K2-1
270 S4=S(J,K+1)+S(J,K-1)
271 S4=S4+S(J-1,K)+S(J+1,K)
275 S4=S4+W(J,K)
280 S(J,K)=S(J,K)*R2+S4*R3
290 NEXT K
300 NEXT J
310 NEXT M
320 PRINT "J";" ";"K";" ";"S VALUE"
322 READ K3,K4
324 FOR K=K3 TO K4
326 FOR J=1 TO J2
328 PRINT J;" ";K;" ";S(J,K)
330 NEXT J
332 NEXT K
400 DATA 10,1.8,11,6
410 DATA 5
420 DATA 3,3
```

```
 400 DATA 10,1.0,11,6
>
 run
fdit.bsc


J K S VALUE
1 3 1.15506855771
2 3 1.285749096132
3 3 1.369227802425
4 3 1.420329012799
5 3 1.450381099844
6 3 1.467401106895
7 3 1.476702579844
8 3 1.481602899464
9 3 1.484044618639
10 3 1.485056863148
11 3 1.375395427385
STOP AT LINE 420
>

 400 DATA 10,1.8,11,6
>

 run
fdit.bsc
```

```
J K S VALUE
1 3 2.02046284525
2 3 1.95524957947
3 3 1.932025283702
4 3 1.941555151373
5 3 1.962606634085
6 3 1.989122029209
7 3 2.028773655158
8 3 2.053602456849
9 3 2.047713970475
10 3 2.038003970967
11 3 2.012506220056
STOP AT LINE 420
>

 400 DATA 20,1.8,11,6
>


 run
fdit.bsc


J K S VALUE
1 3 1.996247247021
2 3 1.998645444442
3 3 2.00409857343
4 3 2.003690300085
5 3 2.001503371761
6 3 2.000213628876
7 3 1.999138181337
8 3 1.999140403851
9 3 1.99947863768
10 3 1.999489464338
11 3 2.000223843962
STOP AT LINE 420
>
```

Program notes

(1) Line 100 dimension arrays S(21,21) and W(21,21). These store the values of stream function S and vorticity W on a grid of up to 21×21 points.
(2) Line 110 reads the data: M1, number of iterations; R1, over-relaxation factor; J2, number of columns in grid; and K2, number of rows in grid.
(3) Line 112 reads H1, the value of S on the top row of the grid. Lines 114 to 116 then set points on the top row to this value.
(4) Lines 180 and 190 find the values of R2 and R3 which are used in the over-relaxation expression.
(5) The iteration starts at line 200 and ends at line 310. Inside this loop, lines 220 to 223 set the horizontal gradient of S to zero on the inflow and outflow boundaries.
(6) The interior points are dealt with in lines 250 to 300. For each of these points the sum of the S values of the four neighbouring

points is found in lines 270 and 271. The vorticity is added to this sum in line 275 but is zero for this problem. In line 280 the latest value of the stream function at the grid point is found using the over-relaxation formula.

(7) Titles for the output are written in line 320. The numbers of the first and last rows to be printed are read in line 322 and for these lines are then printed the column number, row number and S value.

(8) Data for the problem are included at lines 400 to 420.

Example 3.2 FEM2: finite element program for potential flow past a circle

Finite element programs compute values of a function at points on a mesh covering the whole flow field. An example is shown in Figure 3.2, which we will use to calculate the circle flow. It will be seen that the mesh consists of triangles, so it can be fitted to a wide range of shapes. The triangles are called elements, and are the simplest sorts of element we can use. The function is assumed to vary linearly within each. The system of numbering the points (called nodes) at the corners of the triangles is shown. It is different from the finite difference system because the equations for the function will be solved as a matrix and the function values appear as a column vector. In the program FEM2, however, it is assumed that the nodes do lie on a grid system because this allows the node numbers to be allocated to elements automatically. The task of 'mesh generation' is eased by this procedure and the amount of data to be input is reduced. The grid in Figure 3.2 is formed by the radial lines (numbered 1 to 6) and the circumferential lines (numbered 1 to 5). This defines a number of quadrilaterals and the triangles are formed by joining a similar pair of opposite corners in each box. The nodes are numbered sequentially, going through the grid in the order implied by the statements

```
FOR J = 1 TO J1
FOR K = 1 TO K1
```

The equations involving the function ϕ at each node are formed by considering each element in turn. The equations involving the three nodes of each element are assembled into an overall matrix equation. If we go through the 'grid' in the same order as for node numbering, then for each value of J and K in the grid there will be two elements with nodes whose numbers we can find easily from J and K. This is the basis of the program FEM2 listed below.

Lines 10 and 15 set up the arrays needed for the solution. A(30,30) is the matrix of coefficients for the nodal equations, S(30,1) the column vector of the function values for each node, and T(30,1) the right-hand side vector. EA(3) and EB(3) are the terms for the nodes 1, 2, 3 in each element and X(3), Y(3) are the coordinates of the element nodes 1, 2, 3. NN(30,3) are the node numbers which become nodes 1, 2, 3 for each element as it is dealt with, in turn. X1(30), Y1(30) are the coordinates of each node. Line 20 reads in the number of rows and columns in the grid system used for mesh definition and line 21 calculates the number of nodes. Lines 22 and 27 set the matrices to the correct size for the number of nodes and lines 27 to 29 input the node coordinates. Each element in the grid is processed in the loops starting at lines 30 and 31. The node numbers for the two elements in a grid square are found in lines 33 and 34. Then for each of these two elements (NE = 1 and NE = 2) the node numbers for nodes 1, 2, 3 are found (line 50), the terms $\partial N/\partial x$ and $\partial N/\partial y$ are calculated (lines 70 and 80) and the terms in the element matrix equation (3.4) are calculated and added into the main matrix (lines 120 to 170). At line 190 the number of nodes with fixed values of ϕ is read. Lines 200 to 260 then read the node number and ϕ value for each of these points and modify the matrix equation accordingly. If, at node J, S(J,1) is to take value SV then the row J in matrix A has all elements made zero except the diagonal term, which becomes 1.0. The term T(J,1) in the right-hand side vector is put equal to SV.

The matrix equation is then solved in lines 300 and 310 by inverting the matrix A and multiplying vector T by the inverse of A. This is done using the matrix statements available in BASIC on some computers (in this case a VAX). After this the function values found at each node (ϕ or ψ values) are printed (lines 315 to 340). The data start at line 400.

As for reading in the data, the precise system can be seen in the listing. Line 20 reads in J1 and K1, the number of 'lines' in the grid in each 'direction'. Next, line 28 reads in the x and y coordinates of each node, in the order of node numbers explained above. This completes the definition of the boundary shape and mesh. It is clear that the simplification of data input using the grid could be taken a stage further, as only the top and bottom edge of the grid need be given coordinates and the program could interpolate the rest. However, this has been omitted for the present. The next stage of data entry concerns the boundary conditions. In FEM2, the only condition that can be entered is a fixed value of the function (ϕ, say) at a node. If an element side is on the boundary but no condition is imposed on the nodes at each end of this side, then the calculation produces a zero normal gradient condition there. Thus in line 190 the number of boundary nodes with a fixed value is read. Line 210 reads the node number and the function value for each such node.

The data for our test problem can now be discussed. We use the velocity potential, ϕ, as the function describing the flow. The mesh in Figure 3.2 covers a quarter of the flow field, and along the bottom edge and the body surface there is no flow at right angles to the boundary. On these parts of the boundary the condition is $\partial\phi/\partial n = 0$. On the boundary formed by the outer 'circle' of the mesh (nodes 5, 10, 15, 25, 30), ϕ can be fixed at the values it would have in a free stream, i.e. $\phi = U_0x$.

Finally, on the vertical boundary (nodes 26–30) we know that $v = 0$, so $\partial\phi/\partial y = 0$ and we can make ϕ = Constant = ϕ at node 30. These conditions are set up by the data which start in line 400, with the grid dimensions 6 × 5 (J1 × K1). This grid gives 6 × 5 = 30 nodes, so lines 410 to 460 give 30 pairs of x, y values for the location of these nodes. Line 520 gives the number of nodes with a fixed value, which is 10 in our case, and lines 530 to 540 give the node number and value of ϕ for these nodes. The values are $-1.0\ x$, i.e. $U_0 = -1.0$ m/s. The remaining boundary nodes require no data (apart from their positions, already supplied), since the $\partial\phi/\partial n = 0$ condition will then be automatically applied.

The results from these data appear in the form of ϕ values for each node. Picking out the nodes which are on the cylinder (1, 6, 11, 16,

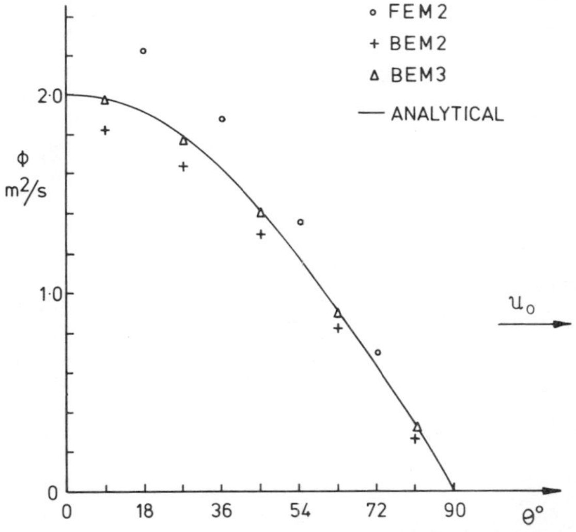

Figure 3.5 Velocity potential calculated by several methods for a circular shape

21, 26) we can compare the ϕ values with the analytical solution $\phi = 2U_0\, a \cos\theta$, which is shown in Figure 3.5. These results are similar in form to the analytical solution but do not agree exactly. This may be due in part to the outer boundary of our mesh being too close. This can be checked fairly easily by moving it, which is a simple matter with the finite element method, and is an exercise which the reader may like to try.

Program FEM2

```
10 DIM A(30,30),S(30,1),T(30,1),EA(3),EB(3),X(3),Y(3),NN(30,3)
15 DIM X1(30),Y1(30)
20 READ J1,K1
21 N2=J1*K1
22 MAT A=ZER(N2,N2)
24 MAT S=ZER(N2,1)
26 MAT T=ZER(N2,1)
27 FOR I=1 TO N2
28 READ X1(I),Y1(I)
29 NEXT I
30 FOR L=1 TO J1-1
31 FOR K=1 TO K1-1
32 NN(1,1)=(L-1)*K1+K\NN(1,2)=L*K1+K+1\NN(1,3)=L*K1+K
33 NN(2,1)=NN(1,1)\NN(2,2)=NN(2,1)+1\NN(2,3)=NN(1,2)
34 FOR NE=1 TO 2
40 FOR J=1 TO 3
50 NP=NN(NE,J)\X(J)=X1(NP)\Y(J)=Y1(NP)
52 NN(NE,J)=NP\X(J)=X1(NP)\Y(J)=Y1(NP)
60 NEXT J
70 EA(1)=X(3)-X(2)\EA(2)=X(1)-X(3)\EA(3)=X(2)-X(1)
80 EB(1)=Y(2)-Y(3)\EB(2)=Y(3)-Y(1)\EB(3)=Y(1)-Y(2)
90 AE=EB(1)*EA(2)-EB(2)*EA(1)
100 FOR I=1 TO 3
110 IR=NN(NE,I)
120 FOR J=1 TO 3
130 IC=NN(NE,J)
140 EK=(EA(I)*EA(J)+EB(I)*EB(J))/2
150 A(IR,IC)=A(IR,IC)+EK
160 NEXT J
170 NEXT I
180 NEXT NE
181 NEXT K
182 NEXT L
190 READ N3
200 FOR I=1 TO N3
210 READ NP,SV
220 FOR J=1 TO N2
230 A(NP,J)=0
240 NEXT J
250 A(NP,NP)=1.0\T(NP,1)=SV
260 NEXT I
300 MAT A=INV(A)
310 MAT S=A*T
315 PRINT "NODE NO.","S VALUE"
320 FOR I=1 TO N2
330 PRINT I,S(I,1)
340 NEXT I
400 DATA 6,5
410 DATA 1,0,1.37,0,1.87,0,2.57,0,3.51,0
```

```
420 DATA .95,.309,1.302,.423,1.78,.578,2.44,.794,3.34,1.03
430 DATA .809,.588,1.11,.806,1.51,1.1,2.08,1.51,2.84,2.06
440 DATA .588,.809,.806,1.11,1.1,1.51,1.51,2.08,2.06,2.84
450 DATA .309,.95,.423,1.302,.578,1.78,.794,2.44,1.03,3.34
460 DATA 0,1,0,1.37,0,1.87,0,2.57,0,3.51
520 DATA 10
530 DATA 5,3.51,10,3.34,15,2.84,20,2.06,30,0,25,1.03
540 DATA 29,0,28,0,27,0,26,0
550 DATA 14,19,18,14,15,19
560 DATA 15,20,18,15,16,20
570 DATA 8
580 DATA 4,-4,8,-3.236,12,-2.082,16,-.927,20,0,19,0,18,0,17,0
600 DATA 7
610 DATA 3,1,6,1,9,1,12,5,15,8.5,14,8.5,13,8.5
```

```
RUN
FEM2

NODE NO.        S VALUE
 1               2.37065
 2               2.50413
 3               2.76091
 4               3.09831
 5               3.51
 6               2.23424
 7               2.36218
 8               2.60697
 9               2.93595
 10              3.34
 11              1.88301
 12              1.99506
 13              2.2052
 14              2.49159
 15              2.84
 16              1.35392
 17              1.43666
 18              1.59524
 19              1.80528
 20              2.06
 21              .703198
 22              .749274
 23              .83013
 24              .942723
 25              1.03
 26              0
 27              0
 28              0
 29              0
 30              0
Ready
```

Program notes

(1) Line 10 dimensions arrays for the calculation. A(30,30) is the matrix of coefficients in the equations for the potential. The potential values at nodes are stored in S(30,1). The right-hand side of the matrix equation is in T(30,1). EA(3), EB(3) are constants in the element shape functions. X(3), Y(3) are the coordinates of the

element nodes. NN(30,3) defines the connection of nodes and elements.
(2) Line 15 dimensions X1(30), Y1(30), the coordinates of the nodes, and line 20 reads in the number of columns and rows in the system of nodes used.
(3) Lines 21 to 26 set the matrices to the correct dimensions for the current problem as required by the matrix solution routine.
(4) Lines 27 to 29 read in the coordinates of the nodes.
(5) The loops from lines 30 to 182 and lines 31 to 181 work through the elements, which are arranged in a grid system to reduce the amount of input data in this program. Lines 32 and 33 calculate the number of the node connected with each element vertex, using the grid system mentioned.
(6) There are two elements in each grid square so line 34 starts a loop to deal with the two elements. This ends at line 180.
(7) The coordinates of each element vertex (there are three) are found in lines 40 to 60.
(8) The constants a_1 = EA(1) are found in lines 70 and 80. The area of an element is then calculated from these in line 90.
(9) Lines 100 to 170 then calculate the coefficients in the local element equations. These are EK in line 140. These EK are added on to the appropriate coefficients in the global matrix A in line 150.
(10) Line 190 reads the number of nodes which have fixed potential values. Their node numbers and potential values are read in line 210. The equations involving these nodes are adjusted in lines 220 to 260. the diagonal term becomes 1.0, all the other terms zero and the right-hand side equal to the potential value.
(11) The matrix equation is solved using the standard matrix routines in lines 300 and 310.
(12) The solution which has been calculated for potential is printed in lines 320 to 340.
(13) Data for the circle flow problem are given in lines 400 to 540.

Example 3.3 BEM2: boundary element program applied to circle flow

The theory of Section 3.7 can be implemented, for the case of constant elements, by the program BEM2 listed below. The dimension statements in lines 10 to 22 allow for the coordinates of both ends of the elements in X(30,2), Y(30,2), the function value ϕ in S(30,1) and the gradient value of $\partial\phi/\partial n$ in F(30,1). The major matrices H(30,30) and G(30,30) correspond to $[H]$ and $[G]$ in Equation 3.11. T1(2), T2(2) are not used in this version of the program; NSF(30) is used to keep account of whether ϕ or $\partial\phi/\partial n$ is the unknown in the final equations; and T(30,1) is used as the right-hand side vector in these equations. FG(6), WG(6) are the Gauss points and weights used in the integration over the elements. At line 30 the data input starts with N1, the number of elements, and M1, the number of integration points on each. Then the integration constants are read. Next the coordinates of the first point on each element, going clockwise round the boundary, are read (lines 35 to 45). The other points are located from these, since the elements must join up. At lines 100 to 131 the matrices are set to the correct size for the calculation in hand. In the loop from line 150 to 310 the equation for each element is worked out, i.e. each row in the matrices $[H]$ and $[G]$. The midpoint of each element is found, then for every other element (loop from 180 to 304) the terms $h_{ij} = \int_{Bi} \partial\phi^*/\partial n \, ds$ and $g_{ij} = \int_{Bi} \phi^* \, ds$ are found.

The length of each element RB and the sine and cosine of its angle to the x-direction are found in lines 200 to 220. Then the integration over the element is done in the loop from line 230 to 286. The coordinates of the integration point are found (line 232), the distance RA to the midpoint of element i (line 240) and the function $T1 = \phi = -\ln(RA)$ are calculated. From line 260 to 280 the orientation of the line from i to the integration point is found (sine and cosine of its angle to x-direction) and the gradient in this direction can be resolved normal to the element j to give $T2 = \partial\phi/\partial n$. The weighted values of T1 and T2 are then added to g_{ij}, h_{ij} to perform the integration. After this the diagonal terms g_{ii}, h_{ii} are calculated (lines 288 to 300).

This completes the matrix equations, and in lines 315 to 330 the boundary values of ϕ and $\partial\phi/\partial n$ are read in. Some of these (half in fact) will be unknown and so are given the value 100. This is the cue, at lines 360 in the loop from 350 to 430, to leave the matrix row unchanged if ϕ (S(I,1)) is unknown, but to swap rows in $[H]$ and $[G]$ if $\partial\phi/\partial n$ (F(I,1)) is unknown, i.e. if ϕ is known. In this way all the unknowns are placed on the LHS and the knowns on the RHS. NSF(I) is made equal to 101 if a swap takes place and the known value of ϕ_i is put in F(I,1).

The matrix equations are now ready to be solved, which is done in lines 550 to 570 using the convenient BASIC MAT statements. Finally, the $\partial\phi/\partial n$ and ϕ values are printed for each element after swapping back the ϕ values known initially into S(I,1), and the $\partial\phi/\partial n$ values solved for into F(I,1) (lines 575 to 620).

The program just described can be used on the same region of fluid as the FEM program to solve the flow round a circle. Elements are only required on the boundary now, so they can be arranged as in Figure 3.4. The data to solve this problem are shown in lines 700–

780 of the listing of BEM2. At line 700, N1, the number of elements, is 18; M1, the number of integration points, is 4. Line 705 gives the integration position and weight for each integration point. Lines 710 to 740 give the *x, y* coordinates of the first point in each element. When one of those is unknown it is given the value 100. The values are assumed constant over the whole element in the theory but also taken as the value at the midpoint of the element, for example in working out the ϕ values in line 750 from $\phi = U_0x$.

Results from the calculation are shown in Figure 3.5. The function does not quite agree with the analytical calculation, and again this may be the effect of a close outer boundary. The outer boundary can be removed altogether if the BEM program is used in another way, described below.

Program BEM2

```
10 DIM X(30,2),Y(30,2),S(30,1),F(30,1),H(30,30),G(30,30)
20 DIM T1(2),T2(2),NSF(30),T(30,1)
22 DIM FG(6),WG(6)
30 READ N1,M1
32 FOR I=1 TO M1
33 READ FG(I),WG(I)
34 NEXT I
35 FOR I=1 TO N1
40 READ X(I,1),Y(I,1)
45 NEXT I
50 FOR I=1 TO N1-1
60 X(I,2)=X(I+1,1)
70 Y(I,2)=Y(I+1,1)
80 NEXT I
90 X(N1,2)=X(1,1)\Y(N1,2)=Y(1,1)
100 MAT H=ZER(N1,N1)
110 MAT G=ZER(N1,N1)
120 MAT S=ZER(N1,1)
130 MAT F=ZER(N1,1)
131 MAT T=ZER(N1,1)
150 FOR I=1 TO N1
160 XI=(X(I,1)+X(I,2))/2
170 YI=(Y(I,1)+Y(I,2))/2
180 FOR J=1 TO N1
200 RB=SQR((X(J,2)-X(J,1))^2+(Y(J,2)-Y(J,1))^2)
202 IF J=I GOTO 300
210 SB=(Y(J,2)-Y(J,1))/RB
220 CB=(X(J,2)-X(J,1))/RB
230 FOR M=1 TO M1
232 RM=FG(M)*RB\XM=RM*CB+X(J,1)\YM=RM*SB+Y(J,1)
240 RA=SQR((XM-XI)^2+(YM-YI)^2)
250 T1=-LOG(RA)
260 SA=(YM-YI)/RA
270 CA=(XM-XI)/RA
280 T2=-(SA*CB-SB*CA)/RA
282 G(I,J)=G(I,J)+T1*WG(M)*RB
284 H(I,J)=H(I,J)+T2*WG(M)*RB
286 NEXT M
288 H(I,I)=H(I,I)-H(I,J)
299 GOTO 304
```

```
300 G(I,I)=-RB*(LOG(RB/2)-1.0)
304 NEXT J
310 NEXT I
315 FOR I=1 TO N1
320 READ S(I,1),F(I,1)
325 NSF(I)=0
330 NEXT I
350 FOR I=1 TO N1
360 IF S(I,1)=100 GOTO 430
370 FOR J=1 TO N1
380 Z=H(J,I)\H(J,I)=-G(J,I)\G(J,I)=-Z
390 NEXT J
400 NSF(I)=101
410 F(I,1)=S(I,1)
430 NEXT I
550 MAT T=G*F
560 MAT H=INV(H)
570 MAT S=H*T
575 PRINT "NODE NO.","S VALUE","F VALUE"
580 FOR I=1 TO N1
590 IF NSF(I)=0 GOTO 610
600 Z=F(I,1)\F(I,1)=S(I,1)\S(I,1)=Z
610 PRINT I,S(I,1),F(I,1)
620 NEXT I
700 DATA 18,4
705 DATA .0695,.174,.9305,.174,.33,.326,.67,.326
710 DATA 3.51,0,3.34,1.03,2.84,2.06,2.06,2.84,1.03,3.34
720 DATA 0,3.51,0,2.57,0,1.87,0,1.37,0,1
730 DATA .309,.95,.588,.809,.809,.588,.95,.309,1,0
740 DATA 1.37,0,1.87,0,2.57,0
750 DATA 3.43,100,3.09,100,2.45,100,1.545,100,.515,100
760 DATA 0,100,0,100,0,100,0,100
770 DATA 100,0,100,0,100,0,100,0,100,0
780 DATA 100,0,100,0,100,0,100,0
790 DATA 100,0,100,0,100,0
800 DATA 100,0,100,0,100,0
```

```
RUN
BEM2          26-MAY-1983 09:15

NODE NO.      S VALUE       F VALUE
 1             3.43         -.894008
 2             3.09         -.755369
 3             2.45         -.609144
 4             1.545        -.373449
 5             .515         -.183469
 6             0             1.13551
 7             0             1.08623
 8             0             1.25549
 9             0             1.67691
 10            .27648        0
 11            .828588       0
 12            1.29902       0
 13            1.64065       0
 14            1.81955       0
 15            1.8625        0
 16            2.05892       0
 17            2.46377       0
 18            3.11743       0
Ready
```

Program notes

(1) Line 10 dimensions arrays for the calculation: X and Y store the coordinates of the two ends of each element; S and F store the potential and its normal gradient at the centre of each element; H and G are the matrices used to form the equations for the unknowns.
(2) Line 20 dimensions some auxiliary arrays: T1 and T2 are used to generate coefficients in the matrix equations; NSF stores a number denoting whether S or F is known on an element; T stores the right-hand side of the final matrix equation.
(3) Line 22 dimensions arrays FG and WG which store the fractions of the element length at which Gauss integration is applied and the weights used in the integration.
(4) Data is read in lines 30 to 45. N1 and M1 are the number of boundary elements and the number of integration points on each. The integration constants FG, WG are read in lines 32 to 34, the coordinates of the first node on each element in lines 35 to 45.
(5) Lines 50 to 90 find the coordinates of the second point on each element. They are made the same as for the first point on the next element.
(6) Lines 100 to 131 give the matrices the correct dimensions for the current problem and set all elements of the matrices to zero.
(7) The loop starting at line 150 and ending at 310 calculates the coefficients in the matrix equations. There is one equation for each boundary element, resulting in a full row in each of the matrices H and G. Every coefficient in a row comes from an integration over a boundary element. These are performed in the loop covering lines 180 to 304.
(8) The length of an element is found in line 200. At line 202 the Gauss integration is bypassed for the element's contribution to its own equation (that is, diagonal terms in the matrices). The sine and cosine of an element's angle to the horizontal are found in lines 210 and 220.
(9) The loop from line 230 to 286 performs the Gauss integration. T1 is the ϕ^* term and T2 the $\partial\phi^*/\partial n$ term.
(10) Line 288 computes the diagonal term of the H matrix by summing the off-diagonal terms. Line 300 calculates the diagonal term of the matrix G directly.
(11) Lines 315 to 330 read in the known boundary values of S (ϕ) and F ($\partial\phi/\partial n$). If S is unknown it is given the value 100. The lines 350 to 430 then swap the row of coefficients in the H and G matrices if S is known on a particular element. The F value will be unknown for this element and the S value is transferred to the F array and note made of this by giving NSF the value 101 (line 400).

(12) The modified matrix equations are solved in lines 550 to 570. Standard matrix routines available in BASIC are used.
(13) Lines 575 to 620 print the solution. Known values of S are swapped back from the F matrix in line 600. The S matrix then contains only values of ϕ and the F matrix only values of $\partial\phi/\partial n$.
(14) Lines 700 to 800 contain the input data. The data given in the listing are for the circle flow problem.

Example 3.4 BEM3: circle flow as an 'external' BEM problem

When the problem of a body in an infinite stream is tackled the BEM need only use elements on the body surface. The trick is to find the solution which has $\partial\phi/\partial n$ equal and opposite to $\partial\phi/\partial n$ in a uniform stream at points where the body surface is to appear. When the solution for the stream is added we will have $\partial\phi/\partial n = 0$ on the body, as required. The only modification to the program BEM2 is that a constant must be added to the term H(I,I) after line 300, because the integration is now round the outside of the elements instead of inside. The new line is

H (I,I) = H (I,I) + 2*PI

The elements must also be numbered anticlockwise for this 'external' type of problem. The program is renamed BEM3.

The same example of flow round a circle can be treated by this method, and the arrangement of boundary elements is shown in Figure 3.6. The input data are given below and the results appear in

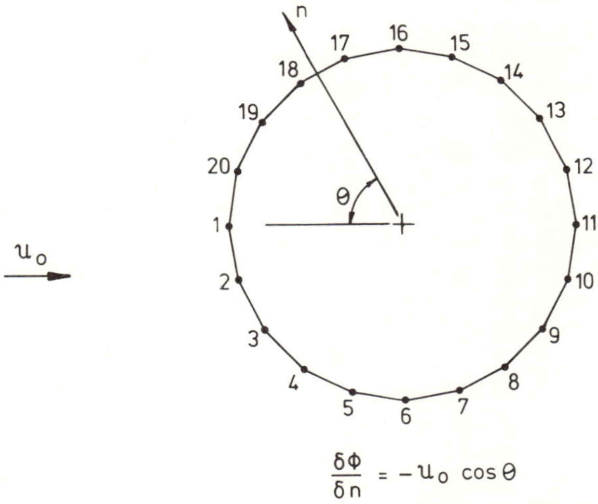

Figure 3.6 Alternative boundary element mesh for a circular shape

Table 3.1. After the uniform stream is added these give the results shown in Figure 3.5, which agree reasonably well with the analytical results.

Table 3.1 Results of BEM – circle flow

θ^0	*Element*	ϕ *calculated*	ϕ *stream*	*Total* ϕ
9	1	+0.9787	+0.9877	+1.9664
27	20	0.8832	0.8910	1.7742
45	19	0.7005	0.7071	1.4076
68	18	0.4496	0.4540	0.9036
81	17	0.1556	0.1564	0.3110

```
700 DATA 20,4
705 DATA .0695,.174,.9305,.174,.33,.326,.67,.326
710 DATA -1,0,-.95,-.309,-.809,-.588,-.588,-.809,-.309,-.95
720 DATA 0,-1,.309,-.95,.588,-.809,.809,-.588,.95,-.309
730 DATA 1,0,.95,.309,.809,.588,.588,.809,.309,.95
740 DATA 0,1,-.309,.95,-.588,.809,-.809,.588,-.95,.309
750 DATA 100,.975,100,.8795,100,.6985,100,.4485,100,.1545
760 DATA 100,-.1545,100,-.4485,100,-.6985,100,-.8795,100,-.975
770 DATA 100,-.975,100,-.8795,100,-.6985,100,-.4485,100,-.1545
780 DATA 100,.1545,100,.4485,100,.6985,100,.8795,100,.975
```

Problems

(3.1) Use the finite difference program to calculate the flow through a tank which is rectangular in shape, 4 m long and 1 m deep. Fluid enters along the first 1 m length of the top surface with a velocity of 1 m/s and leaves through the last 1 m length of the top surface. Find the velocities at the mid-section of the tank and confirm that the flow is evenly distributed through the depth. (The stream function formulation gives the most convenient representation of the boundaries in this case.)

(3.2) Solve a similar problem to (3.1) but with the inflow velocity on the top surface of the tank given by a cosine variation; e.g. $v = \cos \pi\, x/L$. This can be easily checked against the analytical solution

$$\psi = C_2 \sin \frac{\pi x}{L}\left(\exp \frac{\pi}{L} y - \exp -\frac{\pi}{L} y \right)$$

where L = length of tank and h = height of tank

$$\psi = C_1 \sin \frac{\pi x}{L} \text{ on the top surface}$$

$$C_1 = C_2 \left[\exp \frac{\pi h}{L} - \exp\left(-\frac{\pi h}{L} \right) \right]$$

This is also an important solution since it can represent a standing wave in a tank of length $L/2$. If the solution is multiplied by $\sin 2\pi t/T$ it can be seen that water flows down in the left-hand side of the tank and up in the right-hand side from time $t = 0$ to $T/2$, while from $t = T/2$ to T the motion reverses, and so on. The solution also represents the flow round a circle if the coordinates are changed so that the radial and angular positions of a point in the flow are given by

$$r = a \exp \frac{2\pi}{L} y, \quad \theta = \frac{2\pi}{L} x$$

The bottom of the tank now becomes the surface of a cylinder of radius a, the ends of the tank radial lines at $\theta = 0$ and π, and the top surface a large semicircle in the flow, far from the cylinder. The velocities on the cylinder surface can be worked out from the stream function values close to the surface and the grid spacing. They can then be compared with the analytical, FEM and BEM results for the circle flow.

(3.3) Calculate the flow over a flat plate held normal to a stream using the finite difference method and using the velocity potential as the calculation variable. Only one-quarter of the flow field need be calculated due to the symmetry of the flow. This means that the boundaries of the flow fall on a rectangular shape. One vertical side can be taken as the inflow boundary where $\phi = \text{const.} = U_0\, x_1$ (say). The other vertical side will be partly taken up by the flat plate surface, where $\partial\phi/\partial n = 0$. The rest of this face will have $v = 0$, so $\phi = \text{const.} = U_0 x_2$. This value of ϕ comes from the condition $U = U_0$, stream velocity, so $\phi = U_0 x$ on the top surface of the rectangle, which must be far enough from the plate for this to be appropriate. On the bottom side $v = 0$ for the streamline hitting the middle of the plate, so $\partial\phi/\partial n = 0$. The ϕ values and velocities on the plate can be checked using the analytical solution obtained by mapping the circle flow.

(3.4) Calculate the flow through a channel with a sudden reduction in width (sometimes called a bounded step). Use the finite difference program and adapt it to miss out the points in the grid at the corner of the step where the channel reduces its width. The stream function solution will be more convenient to use for the boundary conditions in the finite difference program. The solution can be checked for a ratio of initial to final width of $h_2/h_1 = 0.5$ from the analytical solution of Milne Thomson. On the top surface of the step the velocity is approximately

$\frac{v}{U_0}$	3	2.5	2.05
$\frac{x}{h_1}$	0.039	0.978	0.367

(3.5) In order to examine the problem of modelling curved surfaces the finite difference program using x, y (cartesian) coordinates can be used to calculate the flow round a circle in a stream. The effect of confining the flow by an impermeable boundary may be removed by using the analytical expressions for ψ or ϕ on the outer boundaries of the grid. That is

$$\phi = U_0 \left(r + \frac{a^2}{r} \right) \cos\theta$$

$$\psi = U_0 \left(r - \frac{a^2}{r} \right) \sin\theta$$

The problem is now to fit the circular body surface by points on the regular difference grid. The effect of various schemes to do this on the velocities calculated at the cylinder surface can be examined and compared with the analytical solution for the surface velocity $V_s = 2\ U_0 \sin\theta$.

(3.6) The boundary element method can be used to calculate flows with rectangular boundaries. Compare the results of calculating the flows of questions (3.1), (3.2) and (3.3) with the finite difference and analytical solutions. The simple boundary shapes can be fitted with few elements, but the minimum number for an accurate solution must be found by trial.

(3.7) Carry out the exercise of question (3.6) using the finite element program.

(3.8) More complex curved boundaries can be generated using the program TRANC, together with the analytical solution for the velocities etc on the surface. Calculate the flow round such a shape using the boundary element method. For example, an aerofoil shape or an ellipse can be generated and the x, y coordinates of points on the surface will be output by TRANC; these can then be used as the node points in the BEM data.

Chapter 4

Seepage flows

ESSENTIAL THEORY

4.1 Introduction

The solution methods for potential flow are very useful in problems of flow through porous media. This involves the flow of water through the ground which influences such things as leakage of water from reservoirs, stability of earth embankments, uplift forces on dams and foundations, etc.

The reason that such methods can be applied is that the total head of the fluid satisfies Laplace's equation and is like the velocity potential for irrotational flow. The stream function remains the same as for irrotational flow and so the same solution methods, e.g. flow nets, mapping, numerical methods, are valid.

The equation for flow in porous media is Darcy's equation

$$V = -k\frac{\partial H}{\partial s} \tag{4.1}$$

where V = velocity of fluid
$H = (p/\rho g + z)$ = total head
k = permeability of medium
s = direction of head gradient

V is the mean velocity; that is, volume flow rate divided by area, including area occupied by solid particles. We can see that this is the same as the definition of ϕ in Chapter 2, if we make $\phi = -kH$.

4.2 Confined flow under a dam

The flow under a dam resting on a permeable layer will have the following boundary conditions, referring to Figure 4.1. On CA, the bed of the reservoir, the total head is

$$H_1 = \left(\frac{p}{\rho g} + z_1\right) = \frac{h\rho g}{\rho g} + 0 \tag{4.2}$$

$$\phi = -kh$$

On AB, the bottom of the impermeable dam, $\partial\phi/\partial n = 0$. This is also a streamline of the flow ψ = constant.

The downstream bed BD is another surface of constant ϕ; this time

$$\phi = -kH_2 = -k\left(\frac{0}{\rho g} + 0\right) = 0 \tag{4.3}$$

Finally, the bottom of the permeable layer is represented by a surface on which $\partial\phi/\partial n = 0$. This is also another streamline ψ = constant

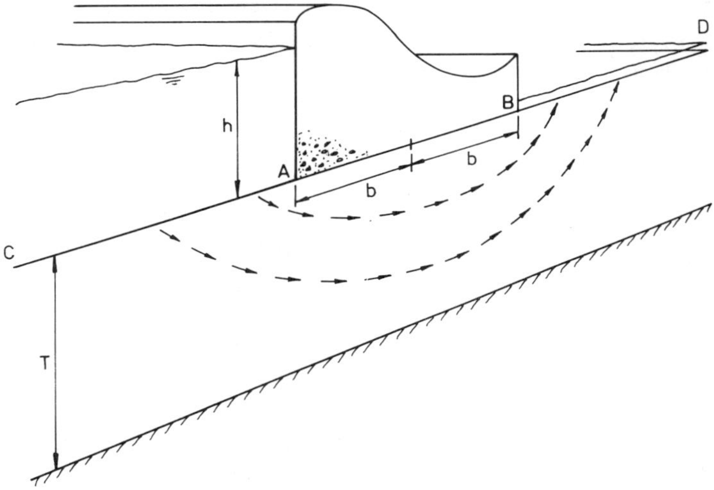

Figure 4.1 Flow under a dam on a permeable layer

The boundary conditions can be represented by the flow net of Figure 4.2, which has the simple equation

$$\frac{x}{b} = \cosh\psi'\cos\phi'$$

$$\frac{y}{b} = -\sinh\psi'\sin\phi' \tag{4.4}$$

where $\phi' = \pi\phi/kh$, $\psi' = \pi\psi/kh$.

We see that the constant ϕ surfaces upstream and downstream are correctly represented by this pattern, as is the flat bottom of the dam. The permeable layer, however, extends an indefinite distance downwards depending on how many streamlines we include in the flow. The effect of a finite width of layer can be simulated by choosing one of the streamlines as the bottom of the layer, so long as it emerges a reasonable distance upstream of the dam, say 2–3 times the dam base width. The distance of the streamline beneath the centre of the dam can be taken as the depth of the layer.

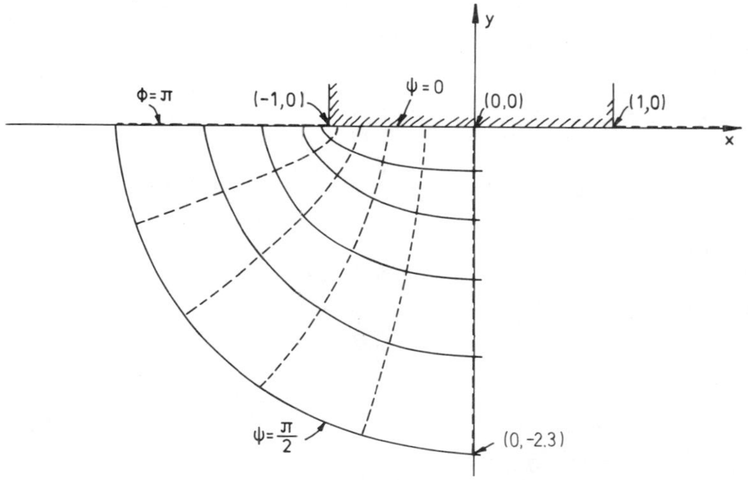

Figure 4.2 Flow net for flow under a dam

There is an exact solution for the finite width of permeable layer by a more complicated mapping and we can use the results of this (see Harr) to compare with various approximate solutions such as that above. Taking T as the thickness of the layer under the dam and b as half the length of the base, the seepage quantity q/kh is shown in Table 4.1.

Table 4.1

$\frac{q}{kh}$ =	0.75	0.53	0.42	0.35	0.3	0.26
$\frac{b}{T}$ =	0.25	0.5	0.75	1.0	1.25	1.5

By the simple flow net $q/kh = N_f/N_e = 0.5$ when $b/T = 1/2.3 = 0.432$. Other cases can be investigated by the equation $q/kh = 1/\pi \cosh^{-1} x_2/b$.

The other quantities of interest are the uplift forces and moments on the structure and the maximum hydraulic gradient at the exit of the flow from the ground. From the exact solution mentioned above it is found that so long as T/b is greater than 1.0 the pressures on the underside of the dam are given very closely by the simple solution for an infinite depth of layer, and these will be on the safe side. From Equation 4.4 the potential on the dam bottom (where $\psi = 0$) is

$$\phi = \cos^{-1} x_1 \tag{4.5}$$

where $x_1 = x/b$. And from the definition of ϕ

$$-k\left(\frac{p}{\rho g} + y\right) = \frac{kh}{\pi}\cos^{-1}\frac{x}{b}$$

since $y = 0$ on the dam bottom and ϕ was assumed zero on the downstream side.

This in turn is quite close to a straight line distribution of pressure between upstream and downstream values, and the total uplift force will be the same if calculated from this simple distribution.

$$p = \frac{h\rho g}{\pi}\cos^{-1}\frac{x}{b} \tag{4.6}$$

The uplift force is in fact

$$F_y = \int_{-b}^{b} p\,\mathrm{d}x = \frac{h\rho g}{\pi}\int_{-b}^{b}\cos^{-1}\frac{x}{b}\,\mathrm{d}x = h\rho g\, b \tag{4.7}$$

The moment of this force is

$$M = \int_{-b}^{b}(x - b)\,p\,\mathrm{d}x = \frac{3h\rho g}{4}\,b^2 \tag{4.8}$$

The exit gradient along the downstream bed

$$i_E = \frac{\mathrm{d}h}{\mathrm{d}y} = -\frac{1}{k}\,\frac{\mathrm{d}\phi}{\mathrm{d}y}\ (\text{on } \phi = 0)$$

This is found to be

$$i_E = \frac{h}{\pi\sqrt{(x^2 - b^2)}} \tag{4.9}$$

It is obvious from the flow net that i_E is very large at the toe of the dam $x = b$, and mathematically it is infinite. The same very high exit gradient applies at the toe of a structure on a layer of finite thickness.

The shape of the boundaries in this problem are suitable for the finite difference method to be applied in a straightforward way. A rectangular region under the dam can be covered by a finite difference grid, and the size of grid can be reduced by covering half the flow area, introducing a constant head boundary on the centre line as indicated in Figure 4.3. The only difficulty arises in deciding how far upstream to place the vertical boundary at the start of the grid. Several positions can be tried and comparison with the exact solutions in Table 4.1 will offer a guide.

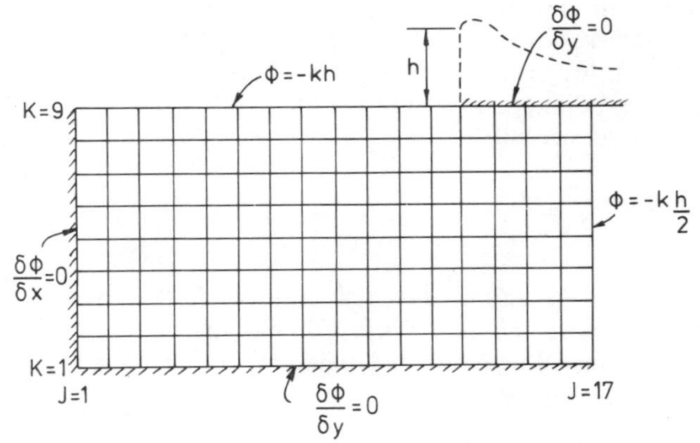

Figure 4.3 Finite difference grid for flow under a dam

4.3 Confined flow into excavations

The quantity of seepage, the exit gradient and the uplift effects may be reduced for dams on a permeable layer by the use of thin vertical barriers formed by sheet piles or grout curtains. Another use of sheet piles is to form a coffer dam to exclude water from an excavation and allow construction in the dry. Some simple examples of seepage flows associated with these uses of sheet piles will now be examined, starting with the single sheet pile.

If a coffer dam is formed by a single sheet pile so that the ground level is the same on both sides of the pile, as in Figure 4.4, the flow net used in the previous section can be turned on its side and used to analyse the problem. The streamline representing the dam bottom becomes the sheet pile and the half-width of the dam b becomes the depth of embedment S of the pile. The quantity of seepage is clearly

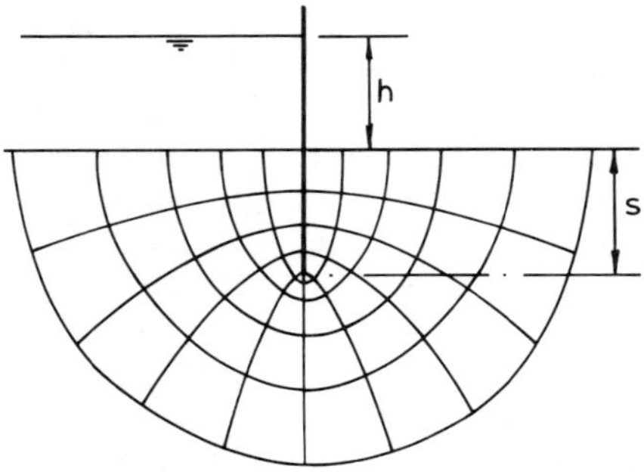

Figure 4.4 Flow net for a single sheet pile

unlimited for an infinite depth of permeable layer, but an approximate result for a finite depth can be found by choosing a streamline as the outer boundary of the flow as in the dam case.

The exit gradient can be found immediately from the flow net and gives the simple result

$$\frac{i_E S}{h} = \frac{1}{\pi} \tag{4.10}$$

For the case of a finite layer thickness, T, this is still a good approximation provided S/T is less than 0.75.

For the ground lower on the dry side of the sheet pile by a distance d, the exit gradient becomes

$$\frac{i_E S}{h} = \frac{Sm}{d(1-m)} \tag{4.11}$$

and

$$\frac{S\pi}{d} = \frac{\sqrt{(1-m^2)}}{m} - \cos^{-1} m$$

For example, see Table 4.2

Table 4.2

$\frac{S}{d}$	0.1	0.2	0.35	0.6	1.0	2.0	4.0	7.0	10.0
m	0.65	0.52	0.4	0.3	0.22	0.13	0.7	0.4	0.35
$\frac{i_E S}{h}$	0.18	0.21	0.24	0.25	0.27	0.29	0.31	0.31	0.31

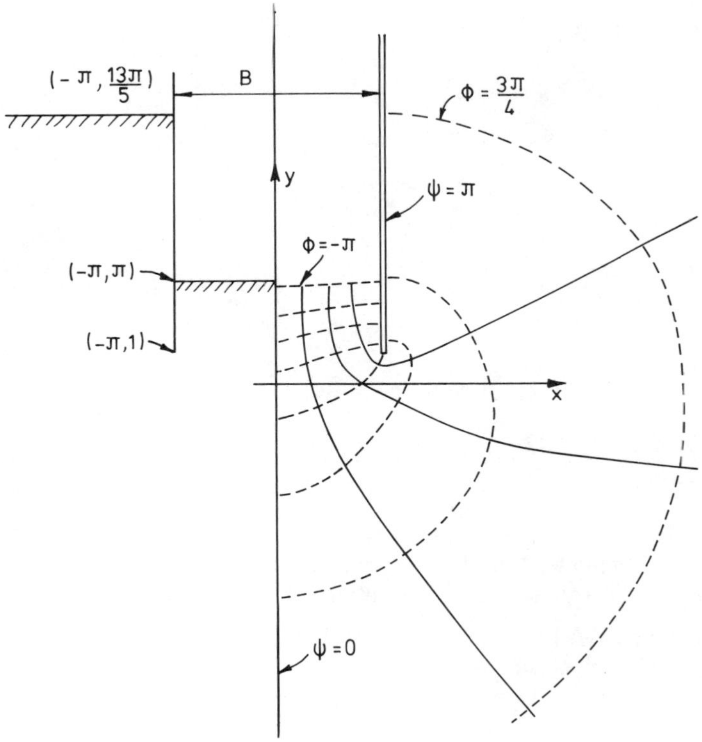

Figure 4.5 Flow net for an excavation between two sheet piles

Often an excavation would be formed between two rows of sheet piles, as in Figure 4.5. The flow net shown in the same figure and given by the equations

$$x = \psi + e^{\phi} \sin \psi$$

$$y = -(\phi + e^{0} \cos \psi) \tag{4.12}$$

approximates to this situation. The quantity of seepage can be found in this case from the flow net ($q/kh = N_f/N_e$), and N_f, number of flow passages and N_e, number of equipotentials, can be found for various depths of excavation d, embedments S and widths of excavation $2b$. An exact solution exists from which the following results in Table 4.3 can be used as a check (see Harr p. 136 for further details).

Table 4.3

$\frac{b}{s}$	0.52	0.92	—	—	—	—
$\frac{s}{b}$	—	—	0.8	1.2	0.5	0.25
$\frac{d}{b}$	1.0	1.0	1.0	0.2	—	—
m	0.02	0.1	0.15	0.7	0.9	0.96
$\frac{q}{kh}$	0.6	0.85	1.0	2.0	2.75	3.5

The average exit gradient at the bottom of the excavation is

$$i_{av} = \frac{q}{2kb} = \frac{N_f}{N_e}\frac{h}{2b} \tag{4.13}$$

The maximum exit gradient occurs close to the piles and will be noticeably higher than i_{av} if the ratio s/b is small; that is, the distance from the bottom to the pile tips is small compared to the width of the hole.

4.4 Flows with variable permeability

In real groundwater flow problems the permeability will often vary from place to place in the flow. For example, the dam or sheet pile of previous sections may be rested on two layers of different permeability. In addition to this, the permeability of the soil may be different in different flow directions. It is relatively common to find situations in which the horizontal permeability is greater than the vertical permeability. In this situation the equation of flow becomes

$$\begin{aligned} u &= -k_x\frac{\partial H}{\partial x} \\ v &= -k_y\frac{\partial H}{\partial y} \end{aligned} \tag{4.14}$$

This is easy for the finite difference and finite element programs to deal with. For example, in the finite difference program we can store two values of permeability k_x and k_y at each grid point and modify the finite difference equation for a typical point as follows.

From Equation 4.14

$$U_{\mathrm{J,K}} = k_x\,(\mathrm{J,K})\,(H_{\mathrm{J+1,\,K}} - H_{\mathrm{J,K}})/\Delta x$$
$$V_{\mathrm{J,K}} = k_x\,(\mathrm{J,K})\,(H_{\mathrm{J,K+1}} - H_{\mathrm{J,K}})/\Delta y$$

And from continuity

$$U_{\mathrm{J,K}}\,\Delta y + V_{\mathrm{J,K}}\,\Delta x - U_{\mathrm{J-1,K}}\,\Delta y - V_{\mathrm{J,K-1}}\,\Delta x = 0$$

so

$$k_x(\mathrm{J,K})\,(H_{\mathrm{J+1,K}} - H_{\mathrm{J,K}})\,\frac{\Delta y}{\Delta x} + k_y(\mathrm{J,K})\,(H_{\mathrm{J,K+1}} - H_{\mathrm{J,K}})\,\frac{\Delta x}{\Delta y}$$

$$- k_x(\mathrm{J-1,K})\,(H_{\mathrm{J,K}} - H_{\mathrm{J-1,K}})\,\frac{\Delta y}{\Delta x} - k_y\,(\mathrm{J,K-1})\,(H_{\mathrm{J,K}} - H_{\mathrm{J,K-1}})\,\frac{\Delta x}{\Delta y}$$

$$= 0$$

If $\Delta x = \Delta y$

$$H_{\mathrm{J,K}} = (C_{\mathrm{N}}\,H_{\mathrm{J,K-1}} + C_{\mathrm{s}}\,H_{\mathrm{J,K-1}} + C_{\mathrm{E}}\,H_{\mathrm{J-1,K}} + C_{\mathrm{w}}\,H_{\mathrm{J-1,K}})/C_{\mathrm{p}} \quad (4.15)$$

where $C_{\mathrm{N}} = k_y\,(\mathrm{J,K})$
$C_{\mathrm{S}} = k_y\,(\mathrm{J,K-1})$
$C_{\mathrm{E}} = k_x\,(\mathrm{J,K})$
$C_{\mathrm{W}} = k_x\,(\mathrm{J-1,K})$
$C_{\mathrm{p}} = C_{\mathrm{N}} + C_{\mathrm{S}} + C_{\mathrm{W}} + C_{\mathrm{E}}$

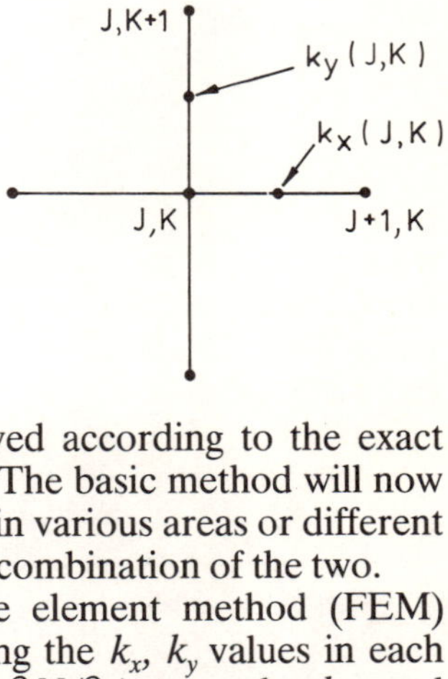

Other similar formulae can be derived according to the exact details of the program being proposed. The basic method will now cover the case of different permeability in various areas or different permeability in different directions or a combination of the two.

A similar modification to the finite element method (FEM) can be made and simply involves storing the k_x, k_y values in each element and multiplying the $(\partial N_i/\partial y)(\,\partial N_j/\partial y)$ terms by k_y and $(\partial N_i/\partial x)(\partial N_j/\partial x)$ terms by k_x as the matrix equation is being formed.

The boundary element method (BEM) is more complicated to adapt to this problem since it requires separate regions surrounded by boundary elements for volumes with different permeability. If the permeability varies with direction then the basic solution used in the BEM to generate the matrix equation must also be modified.

Classical solutions by mapping etc. are few, but some approximate analytical methods illustrate the likely effects and are discussed next. First we can consider a structure on two layers of equal thickness but different permeability k_1, k_2. Solutions may be found for three special cases:

(a) $k_1 \gg k_2$, in which flow is nearly all in the top layer, and for which solutions for a layer of width $d = T/2$ apply.
(b) $k_1 = k_2$, in which the solution for a single layer of width $2d = T$ apply.
(c) $k_1 \ll k_2$, $k_2 = \infty$, no resistance to flow in the bottom layer.

In order to interpolate between the results for these cases the parameter ε is introduced, defined by

$$\tan \varepsilon\pi = \sqrt{\frac{k_2}{k_1}} \qquad (4.16)$$

Thus case (a) gives $\varepsilon = 0$, (b) gives $\varepsilon = 1/4$, and (c) gives $\varepsilon = 1/2$. For a flat-bottomed dam resting on the two layers we can calculate the quantity of seepage. For $\varepsilon = 0$ and $\varepsilon = 1/4$

$$q = k_1 h \frac{K'}{2K}$$

$$\frac{K'}{2K} = \text{function of } \frac{b}{T} \text{ in Table 4.1}$$

$$T = d \text{ for } \varepsilon = 0$$

$$T = 2d \text{ for } \varepsilon = 1/4$$

For $\varepsilon = 1/2$

$$q = \frac{k_1 h}{2}\sqrt{\frac{k_2}{k_1}}$$

E.g., for $b/T = 0.5$

ε	0	0.25	0.30	0.35	0.40
$\frac{q}{k_1 h}$	0.33	0.55	0.7	0.92	(>1.2)

Different permeabilities in the x and y directions can be dealt with by transforming the flow region into one in which the permeabilities are equal and Laplace's equation holds. For example, the equation for flow is

$$\frac{\partial}{\partial x}\left(k_x \frac{\partial H}{\partial x}\right) + \frac{\partial}{\partial y}\left(k_y \frac{\partial H}{\partial y}\right) = 0$$

which may be written

$$k_x \frac{\partial^2 H}{\partial x^2} + \frac{\partial k_x}{\partial x} \frac{\partial H}{\partial x} + k_y \frac{\partial k_y}{\partial y^2} + \frac{\partial k_y}{\partial y} \frac{\partial H}{\partial y} = 0$$

And if

$$\frac{\partial k_x}{\partial x} = 0 \text{ and } \frac{\partial k_y}{\partial y} = 0$$

then

$$\frac{k_x}{k_y} \frac{\partial^2 H}{\partial x^2} + \frac{\partial^2 H}{\partial y^2} = 0$$

or

$$\frac{\partial_2 H}{\partial X^2} + \frac{\partial^2 H}{\partial y^2} = 0$$

if

$$X = x\left(\frac{k_y}{k_x}\right)^{1/2}$$

The problem of flow under a dam could be solved for the case of $k_x = 2ky$ by compressing the flow region by a factor of $\sqrt{2}$ in the x-direction and drawing a normal flow net for the new boundaries. To find the heads in the physical plane, the flow net is stretched back again. The result of this process is shown in Figure 4.6.

To evaluate the seepage flow we can apply an effective permeability to the flow net in the transformed plane.

$$k_e = \sqrt{k_x k_y}$$

$$q = k_e h \frac{N_f}{N_e} \tag{4.17}$$

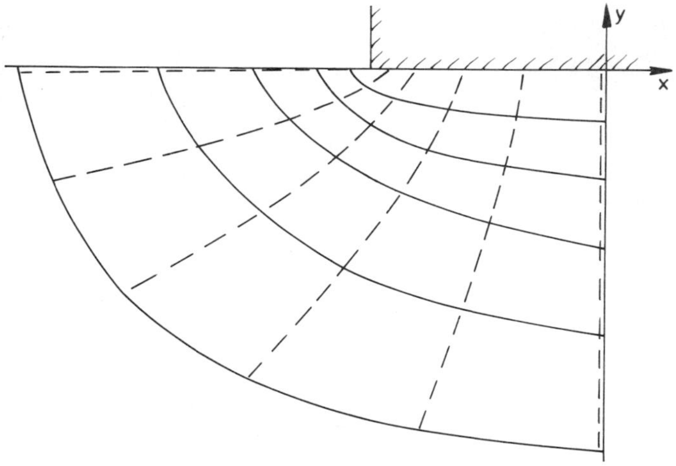

Figure 4.6 Distorted flow net for variable permeability

Alternatively, the head gradients in the physical plane and the actual permeabilities could be used to calculate the seepage flow, and this is the method one would adopt with the finite difference solution.

In the particular example chosen we can see that the heads produced are a little different from the case with equal k_x, k_y. The seepage flow will be increased since k_x is increased, however.

4.5 Free surface flow on a shallow foundation

The problem of seepage through an earth dam is complicated by the fact that the position of the upper surface of the flow is unknown. The boundary condition here is that pressure is atmospheric, which we can write as

$$p = 0$$

so

$$P = \rho g (H - y) = 0$$

Total head

$$H = y$$

or

$$\phi = -ky \qquad (4.18)$$

We thus have a link between ϕ and position on the free surface, and for steady flow the surface is also a streamline.

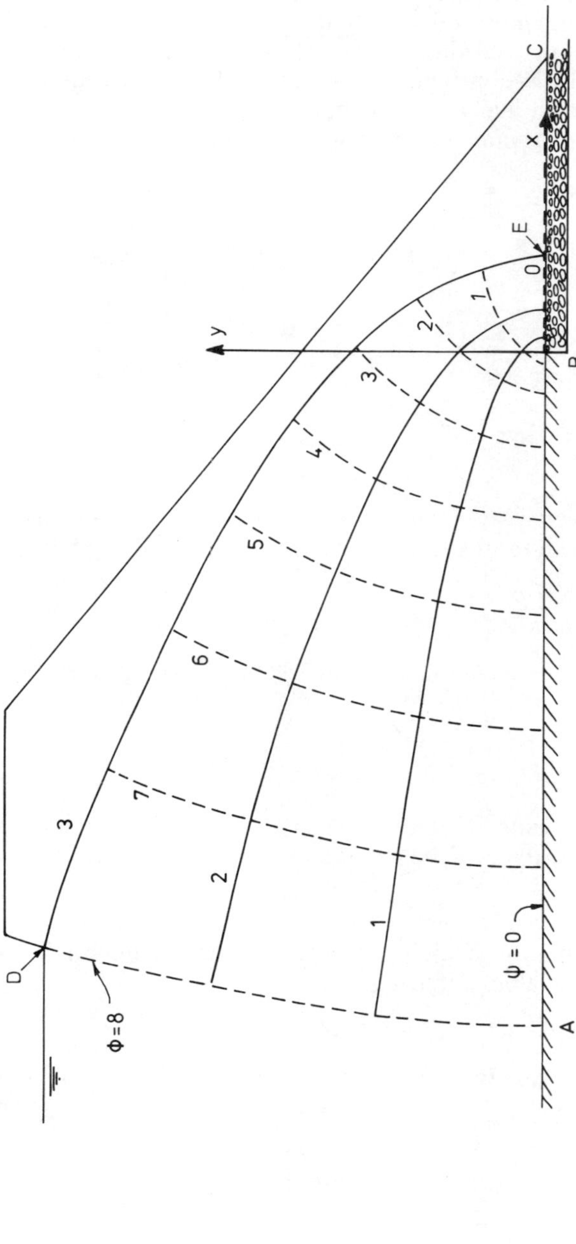

Figure 4.7 Free surface seepage flow to a drain

A problem with a simple solution which illustrates this is the flow through an earth dam on an impermeable layer with a drain in the toe. This prevents the flow issuing from the downstream slope. This is shown in Figure 4.7. On the free surface ED we have $\phi = -ky$ as stated above, and this is also a streamline, $\psi = q$, say. On the toe drain, BC, ϕ = constant, say $\phi = 0$, and on the upstream surface, DA, $\phi = -kh$. Finally, on the bottom surface BA, $\psi = 0$. Kozeny discovered a simple function which satisfied all these conditions

$$\mathbf{z} = C\mathbf{w}^2$$

i.e.

$$x = C(\phi^2 - \psi^2) \qquad (4.19)$$

$$y = 2C\phi\psi$$

From this we see

$$\phi = \frac{y}{2C\psi}$$

That is, on any streamline ψ = constant, we have ϕ = Constant times y, which can represent a free surface. In particular, when $\psi = q$ and $C = 1/-2kq$

$$\phi = -ky$$

This gives the equation of the free surface in our problems as

$$x = -\frac{ky^2}{2q} + \frac{q}{2k} \qquad (4.20)$$

sometimes called Kozeny's basic parabola. The quantity of seepage through the dam can be found by putting $x = 0$, when

$$q = ky_0 \qquad (4.21)$$

And putting this back into Equation 4.20, solving for y_0 and using the x and y values at the upstream end, $y = h$, $x = -d$

$$y_0 = (d^2 + h^2)^{1/2} - d \qquad (4.22)$$

If $y = 0$ in Equation 4.20 the minimum length of the drain is found to be

$$a_0 = \frac{y_0}{2} \qquad (4.23)$$

The slope of the free surface at any point is $-y_0/y$, so arrangements to ensure that the flow does not emerge from any downstream slope can be calculated.

The problem of flow through the core of a dam without tail water also has a simple solution. For a core of triangular section with upstream water level at the apex, as shown in Figure 4.8(a), it can be shown by mapping theory (see Harr p. 201) that for upstream and downstream slopes of 45° the complex potential is

$$\mathbf{w} = \frac{kz^2}{4h} - kh \tag{4.24}$$

i.e.

$$\phi = \frac{k}{4h}(x^2 - y^2) - kh \,/\, \psi = \frac{kxy}{2h}$$

giving the quantity of seepage as

$$q = \frac{kh}{2} \tag{4.25}$$

and the pressure along the dam base as

$$p_0 = \rho g\left(h - \frac{x^2}{4h}\right) \tag{4.26}$$

The expression for seepage flow rate is the same as that found by assuming horizontal flow, which for any slope angle would be

$$q = k\frac{\mathrm{d}H}{\mathrm{d}x}A$$

$$q = \frac{kh}{2}\tan \alpha\pi \tag{4.27}$$

since $A = h$ and $\mathrm{d}H/\mathrm{d}x = \tan \alpha\pi/2$.

A similar result can be shown by more complicated mapping for the case of a vertical upstream face without tail water; here

$$q = kh \tan \alpha\pi \tag{4.28}$$

When there is tail water present, the solution for a triangular section can be found and some results for slopes of 2:5:1 and 3:1 are given in Harr.

For a core with vertical slopes the exact solution for seepage quantity gives results which are very closely approximated by the Dupuit formula, based on the assumption of horizontal flow

$$q = k\frac{h^2 - h_0^2}{2L} \tag{4.29}$$

where h_0 = tail water head.

The height of the exit point of the free surface can be found from the exact solution. For a very thin core, $L/h = 0$.

$$\frac{s}{h} = 1 - \frac{h_0}{h} \tag{4.30}$$

For $L/h > 0$, i.e. thicker cores, s/h is approximately given by

$$\frac{s}{h} = C_1\left(1 - \frac{h_0}{h}\right)^n$$

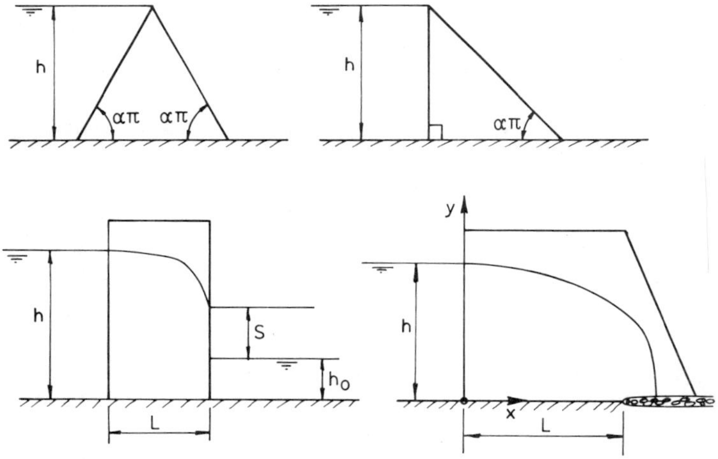

Figure 4.8 Free surface seepage flows in dam cores

with C_1, n given in the table below

$\frac{L}{h}$	0.5	1
C_1	0.62	0.36
n	2	3

Exact solutions are available for earth dams with a given upstream slope $\alpha\pi$ and toe-drain of given slope $\beta\pi$, with various tail water heights, within the drain (see Harr p. 222).

These are quite complicated and only the case of flow through a dam with a vertical upstream face and horizontal underdrain will be given here. The seepage flow in this case is approximately

$$q = k \frac{h^2}{L + \left(L^2 + \frac{h^2}{3} \right)^{1/2}} \tag{4.31}$$

and the free surface is

$$x = k \frac{h^2 - y^2}{2q} - \frac{q}{k} F(\mu) \tag{4.32}$$

where $\mu = \tanh\,[k\pi\,(h - y)/2q]$, and $F(\mu)$ is given by

μ	0.1	0.2	0.3	0.4	0.5	0.6	0.7	0.8	0.9	1.0
$F(\mu)$	0.1	0.17	0.21	0.238	0.26	0.279	0.295	0.308	0.32	0.328

A simple solution for the case of a free surface flow on a deep permeable layer can be given as a last example in this section. The flow is for various slopes of upstream surface towards a horizontal drain, as in Figure 4.9.

The shape of the free surface is given by

$$x = L \sin^{2/n} \frac{\pi y}{2h} \tag{4.33}$$

and the general expression for the flow net is

$$\mathbf{z} = \frac{\mathbf{iw}}{k} + L \sin^{2/n} \frac{\pi \mathbf{w}}{2kh} \tag{4.34}$$

where the shape of the upstream face varies from horizontal to vertical as n goes from 1 to 2. A slope of 45° would be represented by an n value of 3/2 and so on.

The boundary element method is convenient for many problems involving a free surface because the shape of the surface can be followed quite closely by the boundary elements with no special modification to the program. The process of obtaining a solution requires an adjustment to the initial estimate of the free surface position, but only the elements on the surface are moved and there

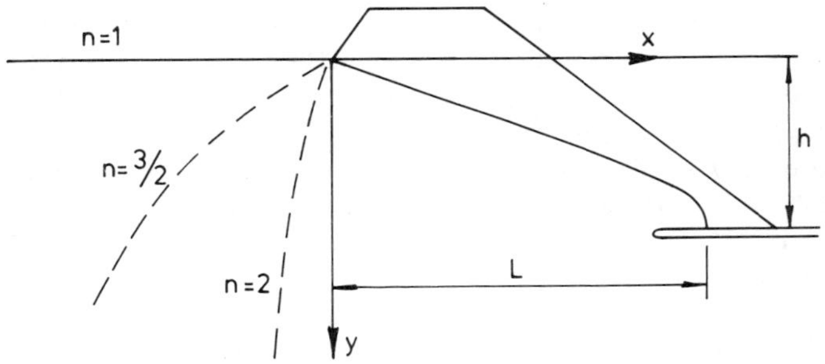

Figure 4.9 Free surface seepage flow on a deep permeable layer (after Harr, *Groundwater and Seepage*, McGraw-Hill, 1962, with permission)

are no internal grid points or mesh points to be moved. These problems can be tackled by simply running the standard program (e.g. BEM2) several times and altering the input data until the desired values of ϕ are produced on the free surface. Usually only a small number (about five) iterations are required to get a reasonable solution.

4.6 Horizontal seepage flow

The flows in a porous medium discussed so far have been in a vertical plane and in a relatively short distance. Another important

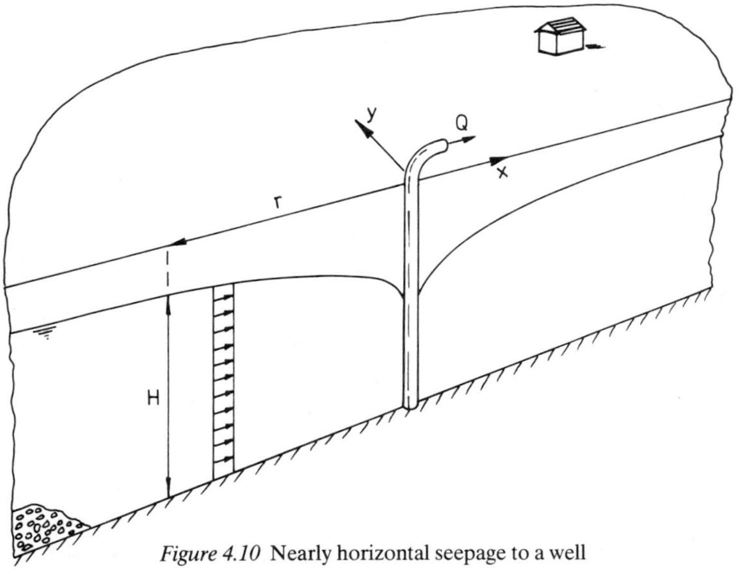

Figure 4.10 Nearly horizontal seepage to a well

class of problems concerns flow in a horizontal plane over a larger distance, usually in connection with the flow towards wells; for example, see Figure 4.10. The flow takes place in a porous layer called an aquifer, which is bounded by an impermeable layer at the bottom and sometimes by an impermeable layer at the top. In the first the flow is termed unconfined and in the second confined. For a confined flow the flow is two-dimensional since the thickness of the aquifer is small compared to its horizontal extent, and the thickness of the flow is constant since the water fills the space between the top and bottom boundaries. The flow in unconfined aquifers can also be considered two-dimensional if the slope of the water surface is not too large. In this case the equipotential lines are nearly vertical and the flow velocity is nearly horizontal and equal at all depths. These are called the Dupuit assumptions for unconfined flow.

4.7 Flow in confined and unconfined aquifers

The equations of flow can be written

$$u = -k\frac{\partial H}{\partial x}, \; v = -k\frac{\partial H}{\partial y}, \; \frac{\partial u}{\partial x} + \frac{\partial v}{\partial y} = 0$$

$$\frac{k\partial^2 H}{\partial x^2} \quad \frac{k\partial^2 H}{\partial y^2} = 0 \tag{4.36}$$

H is the head in the acquifer at point (x, y), or for flow towards a single well

$$\begin{aligned} v_r &= -k\frac{\partial H}{\partial r} \\ v_r &= \frac{Q}{2\pi rT} \\ H &= \frac{Q}{2\pi rTk}\ln r + \text{a const.} \\ H_1 - H_2 &= \frac{Q}{2\pi Tk}\ln\frac{r_1}{r_2} \end{aligned} \tag{4.37}$$

where r = radius from centre of well and T = aquifer thickness.

This is similar to the expression for the potential flow towards a sink. In a confined acquifer we have the expressions

$$\frac{\partial(Tu)}{\partial x} + \frac{\partial(Tv)}{\partial y} = 0 \ , \ T = H$$

so the flow equation is

$$k \ \frac{\partial}{\partial x} \left(H \frac{\partial H}{\partial x} \right) + k \ \frac{\partial}{\partial y} \left(H \frac{\partial H}{\partial y} \right) = 0$$

i.e.

$$k \frac{\partial^2}{\partial x^2} \left(\frac{H^2}{2} \right) + k \frac{\partial^2}{\partial y^2} \left(\frac{H^2}{2} \right) = 0 \tag{4.38}$$

or for flow towards a well

$$H^2{}_2 - H^2{}_1 = \frac{2Q}{2\pi k} \ln \left(\frac{r_2}{r_1} \right) \tag{4.39}$$

We can thus discuss either type of flow in terms of the potential flow theory and solutions available for potential flow if we remember that for confined flow $\phi = -TkH$ and for unconfined flow $\phi = -k/2\ H^2$.

4.8 Well near a boundary

A well near a boundary can be simulated by the use of image wells. A straight boundary with zero flow across it produces the same potential solution as a well plus an identical well discharging at the same rate an equal distance from the boundary position on the opposite side to the original well (see Figure 4.11). A recharge boundary where the head is not changed by the well is modelled by an image well recharging the aquifer at the same rate that the original well draws water out. The drop in head between the boundary and the well of radius r_w for the two cases will be given by

$$\begin{aligned} \phi_B - \phi_W &= \frac{Q}{2\pi} \left(\ln \frac{r_B}{r_W} \pm \ln \frac{r_B}{-r_W + 2r_B} \right) \\ \phi_B - \phi_W &= \frac{Q}{2\pi} \left(\ln \frac{a}{r_W} \pm \ln \frac{a}{2a - r_W} \right) \end{aligned} \tag{4.40}$$

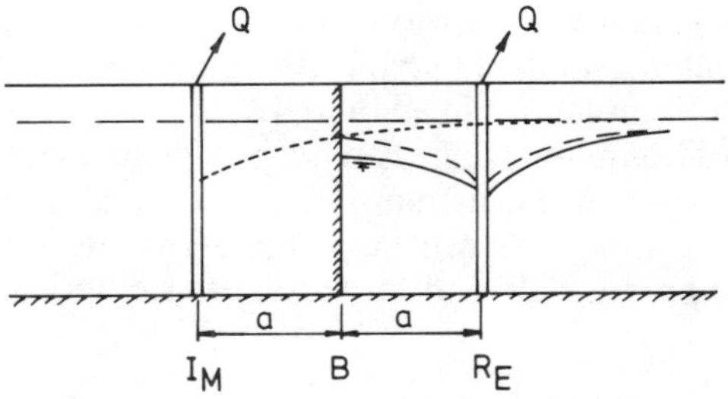

Figure 4.11 Simulation of a boundary by an image well

For the second case the flow pattern consists of circular equipotential lines (see Figure 4.12). These could represent circular recharge boundaries and so the effect of a well at various positions within such a boundary can be investigated.

The position of the image well for a circular boundary of radius R is

$$\theta_i = \theta,\ R_i = r\,\frac{R^2}{r^2} = \frac{R^2}{r} \tag{4.41}$$

The drop in head between the well and the boundary is therefore

$$\Delta\phi = \frac{Q}{2\pi}\left(\ln\frac{R}{r_W} - \ln\frac{\left(\dfrac{R^2}{r} - r - r_W\right)}{\left(\dfrac{R^2}{r} - R\right)}\right)$$

Assuming the same drop in head occurs when the well is at the centre of the region

$$\Delta\phi = \frac{Q_0}{2\pi}\left(\ln\frac{R}{r_w}\right)$$

The ratio of the discharges for various positions of the well can be established as

$$\frac{Q_0}{Q} = 1 - \ln\frac{\left(\dfrac{R^2}{r} - r - r_W\right)}{\left(\dfrac{R^2}{r} - R\right)} \Bigg/ \ln\frac{R}{r_W} \tag{4.42}$$

When this is evaluated for various radial positions of the well, r, it can be seen that the effect of moving the well from the centre is small until the radius is greater than about $0.4R$.

The effect of boundary shape can be investigated by transforming the circular region using a mapping function. For example, the function $\mathbf{w} = C(z + 1/z)$ will map the circle into ellipses if it is centred at the origin. Calculations for various elliptical boundaries

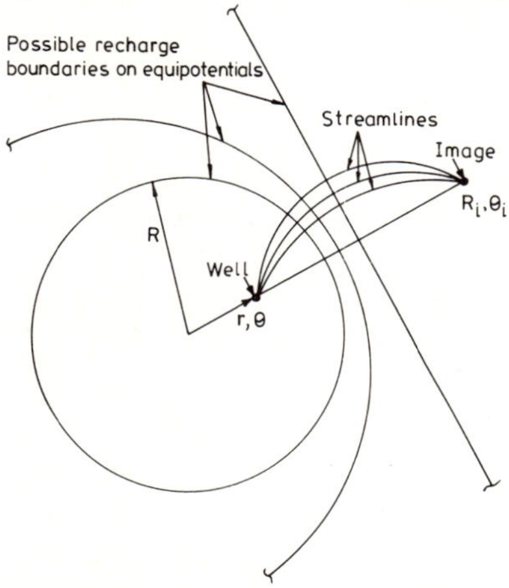

Figure 4.12 A circular boundary represented by an image well

with the same minor axis show that the effect of varying the boundary shape in this way on the flow for a given head drop from the boundary to the well is small. In fact the head drop will be the same in the transformed shape, which has a minor axis given by

$$2Y_{max} = 2C\left(R - \frac{1}{R}\right)$$

and major axis

$$2X_{max} = 2C\left(R + \frac{1}{R}\right)$$

So the radius of the circle is given by

$$\frac{R - \left(\frac{1}{R}\right)}{R + \left(\frac{1}{R}\right)} = \frac{Y_{max}}{X_{max}}$$

$$R - \left(\frac{1}{R}\right) = \frac{Y_{max}}{X_{max}}\left[R + \left(\frac{1}{R}\right)\right]$$

$$R^2\left[1 - \left(\frac{Y_{max}}{X_{max}}\right)\right] - \left[1 + \left(\frac{Y_{max}}{X_{max}}\right)\right] = 0$$

$$R = \left[\frac{1 + \left(\frac{Y_{max}}{X_{max}}\right)}{1 - \left(\frac{Y_{max}}{X_{max}}\right)}\right]^{1/2} \tag{4.43}$$

And, for example, the head drop for a well at the centre would be found from

$$\Delta\phi = \frac{Q}{2\pi}\ln\frac{R}{r_W}$$

Finite differences can be useful in horizontal seepage flow problems. The head is often required at a number of internal points and this is calculated as part of the finite difference process. Wells can be simulated by including a 'source' term, at the nearest grid node to the well, in the finite difference equation. For example, in a regular grid the equation for a node JK with a well discharge at the rate $Q\,m^3/s$ would be

$$\phi_{J,K} = (\phi_{J,K+1} + \phi_{J,K-1} + \phi_{J+1,K} + \phi_{J-K,1} - Q_{J,K})/4 \tag{4.44}$$

where $\phi = -TkH$, for confined flow
$\phi = -k/2\,H^2$, for unconfined flow

The recharge boundaries will be points of constant ϕ on the grid edges, and the no flow boundaries will be nodes at which the condition $\partial\phi/\partial n = 0$ is applied.

4.9 Time varying seepage

The free surface in a seepage flow may change its position with time. An example of this is the water level in an earth dam when the reservoir level is reduced quickly. The water level in the soil cannot immediately follow this change and the water pressure remains high inside the dam, only falling slowly as the water drains out of the interior at a rate which we can find using a time-dependent calculation. At some stage during this process the dam may be liable to a slip failure due to the excess pore water pressures.

Unsteady seepage flow is also important in the case of rainfall on an embankment, which can tend to build up the water level towards the steady state situation and reduce the strength of the embankment. Another problem involving flow into an embankment is the situation where the water level is suddenly raised on one side of it. Cedergren describes the solution of such a problem for a dam on an impervious foundation with upstream and downstream slopes of 1 to 2, a base width of 100 units and a top width of 20 units. The upstream water level is raised from zero to 13 units. The time for the free surface to move various proportions of the base length is given in the table below, expressed as a proportion of the time to cover the whole distance;

$\dfrac{x}{b}$	0.0	0.275	0.44	0.65	0.84	1.0
$\dfrac{t_x}{t_b}$	0.0	0.025	0.1	0.33	0.67	1.0

The time to reach the steady state configuration will be very large, but the free surface will be within 10 per cent of its final height in a time $t/t_b = 1.33$.

The actual time t_b for the free surface to cross the base depends on the permeability k and porosity e of the soil, and the actual base length b. If the motion is divided into a number of steps Δx_n and the hydraulic gradient along the base at each step is i_n then the time for the motion is

$$t_b = \frac{e}{k} \sum \frac{\Delta x_n}{i_n} = \frac{e}{k}\, b \sum \frac{\Delta x_n/b}{i_n}$$

In the problem described, i_n at various x/b is

$\dfrac{x}{b}$	0.1	0.15	0.2	0.3	0.4	0.5	0.6	0.7	0.8	0.9
i_n	6.7	4.7	3.2	1.5	0.3	0.2	0.15	0.1	0.1	0.1

and the quantity $\sum (\Delta x_n/b)/i_n \simeq 60/26.25$.

The finite difference method using iteration is well suited to calculating this type of problem, since the internal flow solution obtained for one position of the free surface is a good approximation to the solution after the surface has moved a short distance. Only a few iterations should be needed to solve for the flow at each time step. The free surface must be moved at each time step and this is done using the equation

$$\frac{\mathrm{d}y_s}{\mathrm{d}t} = \frac{1}{e}(v_s - u_s \tan\alpha) \qquad (4.45)$$

where $\tan\alpha$ = slope of surface $\mathrm{d}y_s/\mathrm{d}x$
v_s = vertical velocity of fluid at surface
u_s = horizontal velocity of fluid at surface.

The solution for potential ϕ or total head H can be found by applying the free surface value of ϕ or H (e.g. $H_s = y_s$) at the nearest grid point to the surface position. The grid points used therefore change as the surface moves and the program must keep track of this. One system is to note the height of each column in the finite difference grid and work through the grid column by column applying the finite difference equation.

4.10 Bibliography

1. Cedergren, H. R., *Seepage, drainage and flow nets*, Wiley (1967).
2. Harr, M. E., *Groundwater and seepage*, McGraw-Hill (1962).
3. Davis, S. N. and DeWiest, R. J. M., *Hydrogeology*, Wiley (1966).
4. Verruijit, A., *Theory of ground water flow*, Macmillan (1970).

WORKED EXAMPLES

Example 4.1 SPXY2: flow under a dam

The position of streamlines and potential lines in the flow under a dam are to be calculated. They can be output as numbers, plotted on the VDU screen and the head output at selected points in the flow net.

The flow net is that of Section 4.2, confined flow under a dam, shown in Figure 4.2. The equation for the flow net is Equation 4.4, which gives the x, y coordinates of a point when the stream function ψ and potential ϕ is specified. The base length of the dam is 8 m and the upstream head 8 m.

The program to find the flow net, SPXY2, is given below, followed by an example of the input for the example problem.

Program SPXY2

```
80  INPUT "TYPE OF FLOW NET";Q%
90  INPUT "FACTOR FOR S,P? ";F1
100  INPUT "S VALUE? ";SP
110  INPUT "P VALUE? ";PP
115 SP = SP * F1:PP = PP * F1
120  GOSUB 1000
```

```
160  PRINT "X COORD.= ";XP
170  PRINT "Y COORD.= ";YP
180  INPUT "ANOTHER POINT?(Y/N) ";A$
190  IF A$ = "Y" GOTO 100
200  GOSUB 2000: REM  PLOT S,P LINES
300  GOSUB 3000
400  STOP
1000  REM  X,Y FROM S,P
1005  ON Q% GOTO 1010,1100,1200
1010 C =  EXP (SP)
1020 CSH = (C + 1 / C) / 2
1030 SNH = (C - 1 / C) / 2
1040 XP = CSH *  COS (PP)
1050 YP = SNH *  SIN (PP)
1060  GOTO 1300
1100 XP = SP +  EXP (PP) *  SIN (SP)
1110 YP = PP +  EXP (PP) *  COS (SP)
1120 YP =  - YP
1130  GOTO 1300
1200 XP = (PP ^ 2 - SP ^ 2) / 2
1205 XP =  - XP
1210 YP = PP * SP
1300  RETURN
2000  REM  PLOT S,P LINES
2010  REM
2020  INPUT "SCALE FACTOR PLOT ";SF
2030  INPUT "X SHIFT           ";XS
2040  INPUT "Y SHIFT           ";YS
2050  INPUT "S,P INTERVAL    ";DP
2055  INPUT "P START         ";P1
2060  INPUT "NO. P LINES     ";N1
2065  INPUT "S START         ";S1
2070  INPUT "NO. S LINES     ";NS
2075 S1 = S1 * F1
2080 P1 = P1 * F1:DP = DP * F1
2090 P2 = P1 + N1 * DP:S2 = S1 + NS * DP
2100  HOME : VTAB 24
2120  HGR : HCOLOR= 3
2140  FOR SP = S1 TO S2 + .01 STEP DP
2150  FOR PP = P1 TO P2 + .01 STEP DP
2160  GOSUB 1000
2170 X1 = XP * SF + XS
2180 Y1 = YS - SF * YP
2190  IF PP = P1 GOTO 2210
2200  HPLOT  TO X1,Y1
2205  GOTO 2300
2210  HPLOT X1,Y1
2300  NEXT PP
2310  NEXT SP
2400  FOR PP = P1 TO P2 + .01 STEP DP
```

```
2410  FOR SP = S1 TO S2 + .01 STEP DP
2420  GOSUB 1000
2430 X1 = XS + SF * XP
2440 Y1 = YS - SF * YP
2450  IF SP = S1 GOTO 2470
2460  HPLOT  TO X1,Y1
2465  GOTO 2480
2470  HPLOT X1,Y1
2480  NEXT SP
2490  NEXT PP
2500  RETURN
3000  REM  SCALES FLOW TO PROBLEM
3010  REM
3020  INPUT "LENGTH OF BASE  ";L1
3025  INPUT "UPSTREAM HEAD    ";H1
3030  INPUT "HEAD DROP        ";HD
3040  INPUT "P VAL.           ";PP
3050  INPUT "S VAL.           ";SP
3055 PP = PP * F1:SP = SP * F1
3060  GOSUB 1000
3064 L2 = L1 / 2
3065  IF Q% = 2 THEN L2 = L1 / 3.1416
3066  IF Q% = 3 THEN L2 = L1
3070 X1 = XP * L2
3080 Y1 = YP * L2
3090 HP = H1 - HD * (PP - P1) / (P2 - P1)
3100  PRINT "X COORD.= ";X1
3110  PRINT "Y COORD.= ";Y1
3120  PRINT "HEAD AT X,Y =";HP
3130  INPUT "ANOTHER PT? (Y/N) ";A$
3140  IF A$ = "Y" GOTO 3040
3150  RETURN
```

```
]RUN
TYPE OF FLOW NET1
FACTOR FOR S,P? 3.1416
S VALUE? 0
P VALUE? 1
X COORD.= -1
Y COORD.= 0
ANOTHER POINT?(Y/N) Y
S VALUE? .5
P VALUE? 1
X COORD.= -2.50918693
Y COORD.= -1.6907192E-05
ANOTHER POINT?(Y/N) Y
S VALUE? .5
P VALUE? 1.5
X COORD.= 2.76553169E-05
```

```
Y COORD.= -2.30130812
ANOTHER POINT?(Y/N) N
SCALE FACTOR PLOT 50
X SHIFT          200
Y SHIFT           10
S,P INTERVAL     .05
P START          1
NO. P LINES      10
S START          0
NO. S LINES      10
LENGTH OF BASE   8
UPSTREAM HEAD     8
HEAD DROP        4
P VAL.           1.25
S VAL.           0
X COORD.= -2.82840115
Y COORD.= 0
HEAD AT X,Y =6
ANOTHER PT? (Y/N) N
```

Program notes

(1) Line 80 inputs the type of flow net required, Q%. If Q% = 1 the flow net for the dam is calculated, if Q% = 2 the flow between two sheet piles, and if Q% = 3, the free surface flow to a drain.
(2) In line 90 a factor for the stream function ψ and velocity potential ϕ is input. This is used to avoid inputting multiples of π. For example, if it is desired to make $\phi = 0.5\pi$ the value 0.5 is input instead of 1.5708.
(3) Lines 100 and 110 input the values of ψ and ϕ required; these are denoted by SP and PP in the program. Line 115 applies the factor to these values and at line 120 subroutine 1000 is called to calculate the x, y position of this point in the flow net.
(4) Lines 160 to 190 print the x and y coordinates and give an option to calculate another point. This first part of the program is used to check up on the size of the plot needed. The flow net is plotted on the VDU screen by subroutine 2000, called at line 200.
(5) At line 300 the subroutine 3000 is called, which calculates the head and x, y position at points in the particular size of problem specified; the flow net being scaled up to fit, for example, the base length of the dam actually chosen. The program finishes at line 400.
(6) In subroutine 1000 x, y positions are calculated for ψ, ϕ values. In line 1005 the type of flow net required is recognized from the value of Q%. If Q% = 1, lines 1010 to 1050 calculate the coordinates in the dam flow net. If Q% = 2 lines 1110 to 1120 are used to find the coordinates in the sheet-pile flow net, and if Q% = 3 lines 1200 to 1210 calculate the free surface flow net.

(7) In subroutine 2000 streamlines and potential lines are plotted. At line 2020 a scale factor for the plot is input, and at lines 2030 and 2040 the shifts in the *x* and *y* coordinates. These three quantities are needed to fit the flow net in the 360 × 160 pixel space on the screen.
(8) Lines 2050 to 2070 input the quantities describing the flow net: DP is the interval in ϕ and ψ values between neighbouring lines; P1 is the ϕ value on the first ϕ line; and N1 the number of ϕ lines. S1 is the ψ value on the first ψ line and NS the number of ψ lines.
(9) Lines 2075 to 2090 multiply DP etc. by the factor for ψ and ϕ input at line 90. The values of ψ and ϕ on the last lines are also calculated.
(10) Lines 2100 and 2120 set up the screen for plotting.
(11) Lines 2140 to 2310 plot the streamlines in the flow net. Lines 2160 to 2180 calculate the *x, y* position of a point on a streamline. If this is the first point on that line then the program goes to line 2210 and a dot is plotted, otherwise a line is drawn from the previous point.
(12) Lines 2400 to 2490 plot the potential lines in the flow net, by a similar procedure to that used for streamlines.
(13) The subroutine 3000 calculates *x, y* coordinates and total head in the flow net scaled up to the problem size. Line 3020 inputs a base length, L1. This is the base length of the dam or the distance between sheet piles. A value of 1.0 can be used for the free surface flow. Lines 3025 and 3030 input the actual upstream head H1 and the head drop across the whole flow net. Lines 3040 and 3050 input the ψ and ϕ value at the point in the flow net required.
(14) Line 3055 multiplies ψ and ϕ values by the factor, and line 3060 finds the *x, y* position in the original flow net.
(15) Lines 3064 to 3066 calculate the scaling factor L2 for increasing the flow net to the size of the real problem.
(16) The actual *x, y* coordinates of the ψ, ϕ point are found in lines 3070 and 3080, and the actual total head at this point at line 3090. These values are printed in lines 3100 to 3120. The option to calculate another point is given in lines 3130 to 3140.

Example 4.2 XYSP2: flow to wells on an island

The positions of ϕ and ψ lines are not straightforward to plot, but the values of ϕ at various positions can be found simply by adding the solutions for the various wells and images. A program to do this and print values at chosen points is given below. It is called XYSP2. An example calculation, which can also be solved later using the finite difference method, is given to illustrate the use of XYSP2.

The problem to be considered is that of a square island which has a permeability of 0.033 m/day and rests on an impermeable bed in water of depth 30 m. This is shown in Figure 4.13. In the middle of the island are four wells which are used to lower the groundwater level for an excavation. We are required to find the rate of pumping to reduce the depth of flow to 25 m, inside the area bounded by the wells.

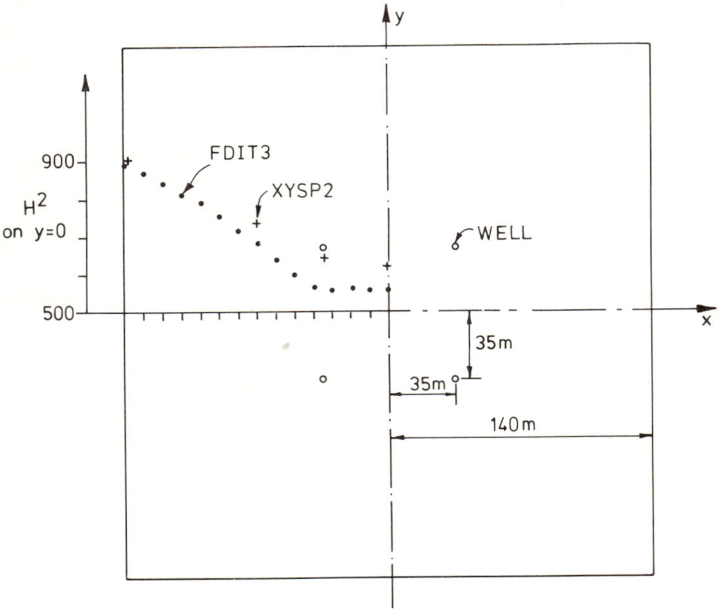

Figure 4.13 Calculations of flow to four wells in a square island

Recall that we are solving for H^2, so this has a value of $30^2\,m^2 = 900\,m^2$ at the edges of the island. The well flow is adjusted until the water levels in the square bounded by the wells are all below 25 m (i.e. $H^2 = 625\,m^2$).

The problem may be solved approximately by simply using the four wells in the solution. This will give a curved boundary of constant head rather than a square, but the solution will not be greatly different near the wells. We actually solve the problem by choosing a flow rate and working out the difference in ϕ between the centre of the island and the edge, $\Delta\phi$. This is converted to a difference in H^2, ΔH^2. The final flow rate required is found by multiplying the chosen flow rate by the ratio (ΔH^2 required)/(ΔH^2 found) since the equation for H^2 is linear. If the head at a point in the island is required we find the difference in H^2 between the edge and the point from the solution and add the known value of H^2 at the edge (900 m^2) to get the value of H^2 at the point. For example, using the program XYSP2, we can input the data shown after the program listing.

We take the flow from each well to be $Q/2\pi = 0.5\,\text{m}^3/\text{day}$. The program gives us values of ϕ which we convert to head^2 from $H^2 = 2\phi/k$. Values of ϕ are requested at $x = 140$ m, $y = 0$ m and $x = 0$ m in response to the prompt; that is, at the edge of the island and in the centre at the middle of the excavation. The results are $\phi = 9.8\,\text{m}^2/\text{day}$ and $\phi = 7.80\,\text{m}^2/\text{day}$. The difference in ϕ between the centre of the excavation and the edge of the island is $\Delta\phi = 9.89 - 7.80 = 2.09$. So

$$\Delta H^2 = \frac{2.09 \times 2}{0.003} = 125.4\,\text{m}^2$$

But we actually require $\Delta H^2 = 900 - 625 = 275\,\text{m}^2$, so flow required

$$Q = (0.5 \times 2\pi) \times \frac{275}{125.4} = 7.12\,\text{m}^3/\text{day}$$

(since there is a linear relationship between $\Delta\phi$ and Q).

Program XYSP2

```
100  DIM XS(10),YS(10),QS(10)
110  INPUT "NO. OF WELLS? ";NW
112  FOR I = 1 TO NW
120  INPUT "X SOURCE";XS(I)
130  INPUT "Y SOURCE";YS(I)
140  INPUT "Q/2PI SOURCE";QS(I)
142  NEXT I
150  INPUT "X COORD. ";XP
160  INPUT "Y COORD. ";YP
170  GOSUB 1400: REM  FIND S,P
230  PRINT "STREAM FUNC.= ";ST
240  PRINT "VEL. POT.= ";PT
250  INPUT "ENTER Y TO REPEAT- ";A$
260  IF A$ = "Y" GOTO 150
270  STOP
1400  REM  FINDS S,P
1405 PT = 0:ST = 0
1410  FOR I = 1 TO NW
1420 XS = XS(I)
1430 YS = YS(I)
```

```
1440 QS = QS(I)
1500 DX = XP - XS
1510 DY = YP - YS
1515  IF DY = 0 THEN DY = .001
1520 RS = DX ^ 2 + DY ^ 2
1530 T2 =  ATN (DX / DY)
1540 T1 = T2 + 1.5708
1550  IF DY < 0 THEN T1 = T2 + 4.7124
1560 SP =  - QS * T1
1570 PP = QS *  LOG (RS) / 2
1580 ST = ST + SP
1590 PT = PT + PP
1600  NEXT I
1610  RETURN
```

```
]RUN
NO. OF WELLS? 4
X SOURCE35
Y SOURCE35
Q/2PI SOURCE.5
X SOURCE-35
Y SOURCE35
Q/2PI SOURCE.5
X SOURCE-35
Y SOURCE-35
Q/2PI SOURCE.5
X SOURCE35
Y SOURCE-35
Q/2PI SOURCE.5
X COORD. 0
Y COORD. 0
STREAM FUNC.= -6.2832
VEL. POT.= 7.80384331
ENTER Y TO REPEAT- Y
X COORD. 140
Y COORD. 0
STREAM FUNC.= -6.2832
VEL. POT.= 9.89103694
ENTER Y TO REPEAT- Y
X COORD. 140
Y COORD. 140
STREAM FUNC.= -4.71239633
```

Program notes

(1) Line 100 dimensions arrays to store the details of up to 10 wells. XS(10) and YS(10) are the *x* and *y* coordinates of the wells and QS(10) the flows into each well.

(2) Line 110 inputs the number of wells. In lines 112 to 140 the x and y coordinates and the flow QS expressed as $Q/2\pi$ are input for each well.
(3) In lines 150 and 160 the x and y coordinates of the point at which the stream function ST and potential PT are due to the well are input.
(4) At line 170 the subroutine 1400 to find ST and PT is called. These values are then printed in lines 230 and 240. The calculation can be repeated for another point by typing Y in response to the prompt at line 250 and the program ends at line 270.
(5) The subroutine 1400 finds ST and PT. At line 1405 the totals ST and PT are set to zero. In lines 1410 to 1600 the contributions from each well to ST and PT are calculated and added to the running totals. The process is the same as for the calculation of the source in program XYSP1 (Chapter 2).

Example 4.3 FDIT3: flow to wells – finite differences

The program used in the last section can be repeated using finite differences. Only one-quarter of the island need be considered from the symmetry of the problem, which saves some calculation. The method of solution is similar to FDIT1 of Chapter 3 except that a 'source' term W(J,K) is introduced into the finite difference equation. This is zero except at the node nearest the well. The grid squares are given a side of 10m and the boundary conditions indicated below applied.

A listing of the finite difference program is given below. It is called FDIT3 and is very similar to FDIT1, the changes being to set the boundary values at the top and right-hand edges of the grid, in lines 114 to 119, and also the reading of the well position, the discharge and the permeability at lines 120 and 122, and the inclusion of the source term in the equations at line 275. The normal gradient of H^2 is set equal to zero on the bottom and left-hand sides of the grid by including lines 210 and 220 in the iteration procedure. The 'source' term in the equation will be

$$W_{\mathrm{J,K}} = \frac{2q\Delta x^2}{k} = \frac{2Q}{k}$$

where Q= flow from well, k= permeability.

So in the calculation shown, $k = 0.033\,\mathrm{m/day}$, $Q = 6.66\,\mathrm{m^3/day}$, $W_{\mathrm{J,K}} = 4 \times 10^2\,\mathrm{m^2}$, as shown in the data at line 420.

The results printed are the values of H^2 on the rows of the grid specified in the input data. The grid coordinates J, K and the H^2

value are printed in a table with three columns. These have been plotted in Figure 4.13 where it can be seen that the water level has been reduced sufficiently by the flow chosen. This flow is also approximately equal to the flow estimated from the analytical solution of Example 4.2.

Program FDIT3

```
100  DIM S(21,21),W(21,21)
110  READ M1,R1,J2,K2
112  READ H1
114  FOR J = 1 TO J2
115 S(J,K2) = H1
116  NEXT J
117  FOR K = 1 TO K2
118 S(J2,K) = H1
119  NEXT K
120  READ JW,KW,WV
122 W(JW,KW) = WV
180 R2 = 1.0 - R1
190 R3 = R1 / 4
200  FOR M = 1 TO M1
202  PRINT "ITERATION ";M;" OF ";M1
210  FOR J = 1 TO J2
211 S(J,1) = S(J,2)
212  NEXT J
220  FOR K = 1 TO K2
221 S(1,K) = S(2,K)
222  NEXT K
250  FOR J = 2 TO J2 - 1
260  FOR K = 2 TO K2 - 1
270 S4 = S(J,K + 1) + S(J,K - 1)
271 S4 = S4 + S(J + 1,K) + S(J - 1,K)
275 S4 = S4 + W(J,K)
280 S(J,K) = S(J,K) * R2 + S4 * R3
290  NEXT K
300  NEXT J
310  NEXT M
320  PRINT "J","K","S VALUE"
322  READ K3,K4
324  FOR K = K3 TO K4
326  FOR J = 1 TO J2
328  PRINT J,K,S(J,K)
330  NEXT J
332  NEXT K
400  DATA   50,1.8,15,15
410  DATA  900
420  DATA   5,5,-4E2
430  DATA  1,4
```

Program notes

(1) Line 100 dimensions arrays S(21,21) and W(21,21) to store the potential and inflow at each of the grid points in a finite difference grid.
(2) Line 110 reads the data controlling the solution procedure. M1 is the number of iterations, R1 the over-relaxation factor, J2 and K2 the number of columns and rows in the finite difference grid.
(3) Line 112 reads the potential at the outer edge of the island. The top row and end columns of the grid are set to this value in lines 114 to 119.
(4) At line 120 the location of the nearest grid point to the well and its flow WV are read. This flow is stored in W(JW, KW) in line 122.
(5) Lines 180 and 190 calculate constants which will be used in the iteration procedure. This starts at line 200 and includes the lines up to 310.
(6) A message to show the progress of the iteration is printed at line 202.
(7) In lines 210 to 222 the first (left-hand) column and bottom row of the grid have the zero gradient condition for potential applied to them.
(8) Lines 250 to 300 calculate the potential at all interior points in the grid using the standard finite difference equation.
(9) Lines 320 to 332 print the potential values at grid points selected in line 322. The values are on the grid rows between the row numbers K3 and K4.
(10) The data for the square island problem are given in lines 400 to 430.

Example 4.4 FDIT10: flow under a dam – finite differences

The finite difference program for Laplace's equation introduced in Chapter 3, FDIT1, can also be adapted to solve this case. Instead of the stream function we use the total head as the calculation variable and this results in the boundary conditions shown in Figure 4.3. We have taken only the left-hand half of the fluid region since the right-hand half will be similar and the permeable layer has been stopped 16 m from the centre of the dam.

On the impermeable surfaces the normal velocity is zero and from Darcy's Law the normal gradient of H is also zero. On the bottom of the reservoir H equals the pressure head h plus y. Taking $y = 0$ at this level $H = h$. On the downstream side of the dam $H = 0$ so on the line of symmetry $H = H/2$.

The program FDIT10 is given below. The solution of the equation for H is by the same iterative method as in FDIT1 but the name S(J,K) is now used for H. The new boundary conditions are imposed in a similar way by either leaving H values on the boundary unchanged at the fixed boundary values or changing them to give zero gradients where required. The data input is by input statements, asking for the dimensions of the problem area, number of iterations, etc.

The input required for the problem is also shown after the listing. Output is simply the H values on a horizontal line of grid points which the user selects. The line immediately under the dam and the ground surface is obviously of interest and this is shown in Table 4.4.

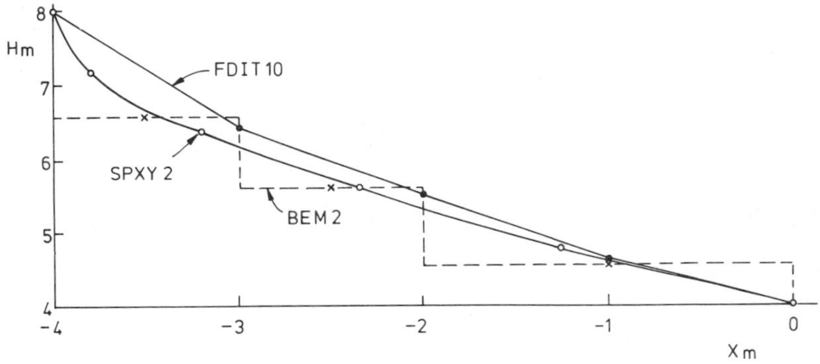

Figure 4.14 Head on the base of a dam calculated by several methods

It is easier to compare the analytical and finite difference solutions on a plot of H against x. This is shown in Figure 4.14, where it can be seen that the two solutions agree quite well. The hydraulic gradient $i = \partial H/\partial y$ at the heel and toe points is approximately 1.0 in the numerical solution, i.e. near the critical value but not so high as the analytical solution. The depth of the permeable layer under the middle of the dam is 9.2 m in the analytical solution compared to 8 m in the finite difference grid. This is because the ψ values were chosen at the nearest convenient value for the analytical solution.

Program FDIT10

```
100  DIM S(21,21),W(21,21)
102  INPUT "NO. COLUMNS ";J2
103  INPUT "NO. ROWS    ";K2
104  INPUT "UPSTREAM HEAD ";H1
110  INPUT "NO. ITERS";M1
```

```
111  INPUT "O/RELAX. FACTOR ";R1
114  FOR J = 1 TO J2
115 S(J,K2) = H1
116  NEXT J
117  FOR K = 1 TO K2
118 S(J2,K) = H1 / 2
119  NEXT K
120  INPUT "START OF DAM ";J3
122 J4 = J2 - 1
180 R2 = 1.0 - R1
190 R3 = R1 / 4
200  FOR M = 1 TO M1
202  PRINT "ITERATION ";M;" OF ";M1
210  FOR J = 1 TO J2
211 S(J,1) = S(J,2)
212  NEXT J
220  FOR K = 1 TO K2
221 S(1,K) = S(2,K)
222  NEXT K
229 K = K2
230  FOR J = J3 TO J4
232 S(J,K2) = (S(J,K - 1) * 2 + S(J + 1,K) + S(J
234  NEXT J
250  FOR J = 2 TO J2 - 1
260  FOR K = 2 TO K2 - 1
270 S4 = S(J,K + 1) + S(J,K - 1)
271 S4 = S4 + S(J + 1,K) + S(J - 1,K)
280 S(J,K) = S(J,K) * R2 + S4 * R3
290  NEXT K
300  NEXT J
310  NEXT M
320  INPUT "ROW TO BE PRINTED? ";K
325  PRINT "COL. NO.","POTENTIAL ROW ";K
326  FOR J = 1 TO J2
328  PRINT J,S(J,K)
330  NEXT J
332  INPUT "TYPE Y FOR ANOTHER ROW ";A$
334  IF A$ = "Y" GOTO 320
400  INPUT "TYPE Y FOR MORE ITERS ";A$
410  IF A$ = "Y" GOTO 200
500  STOP
```

Program notes

(1) At line 100 arrays S(21,21) and W(21,21) are dimensioned. S stores the potential or head values at the nodes of the finite difference grid and W is not used in this example.

(2) From lines 102 to 111 the basic data are input. J2, K2 are the number of columns and rows in the grid. H1 is the head upstream of the dam. M1 is the number of iterations and R1 the over-relaxation factor.
(3) The lines 114 to 119 set the head value to H1 on the top row of the grid and to H1/2 on the right-hand column. Part of the top row will take different values later since it represents the bottom of the dam. The *x* coordinate of the start of the dam is input at line 120.
(4) Various constants are calculated in lines 122 to 190. These are J4, the last grid column included in the iteration, and R2 and R3, involved in the over-relaxation at line 280.
(5) At line 200 the main iteration starts. Line 202 prints a message to show the progress of the iteration. Lines 210 to 222 make the head gradient zero normal to the bottom boundary and the left-hand boundary.
(6) Lines 229 to 234 make the head gradient zero normal to the dam bottom. This is done by applying a special version of the finite difference equation as in Chapter 3. No over-relaxation is used.
(7) Lines 250 to 300 apply the standard finite difference form of the Laplace equation at all the internal points. Over-relaxation is used at line 280.
(8) Results are output in lines 320 to 334. The head is printed on the row of the grid selected at line 320. The column number and head value are printed in lines 325 to 330. An option to print another row is given in lines 332 and 334.
(9) A further M1 iterations can be selected in lines 400 and 410. The program ends at line 500.

Example 4.5 FDIT12: seepage with varying permeability – finite differences

The permeabilities k_x, k_y are often variable from place to place in a seepage flow. This aspect of the problem can be included in a method of solution which stores the flow variable at points inside the flow region; for example the finite difference method. The finite difference equation will be modified by variable permeabilities in the way shown in Section 4.4.

This is the modified finite difference equation employed in the program FDIT12, listed below. The permeabilities can be read in by assigning k_x, k_y values to blocks of points as in lines 130 to 150. Two examples are calculated, based on the flow under a dam. The boundaries have the same form as in the last example. In the first case the horizontal permeability $k_x = 2$ m/d but the vertical permeability $k_y = 1$ m/d. Values of head along the base of the dam calculated by the program are shown in Table 4.4. They are very similar to the results for constant permeability $k_x = k_y = \text{const.}$ (The analytical solution gives the same head on the dam base as with constant k.)

The second example has the dam resting on two permeable layers, the upper one from $y=0$ to $y=-3$ m with $k=1$ m/d and the lower from $y=-4$ m to $y=-8$ m with $k=0.5$ m/d. The head on the dam bottom again is not changed dramatically and neither are the head gradients on the vertical line under the dam. The flow under the dam will be reduced below the case with $k_x = 1$ m/d everywhere, because the permeability in the lower layer is reduced. Thus the flow found from $q = \int^{-8}_{0} k_x\,(dH/dx)\,dy$ is less.

The values of head on a vertical line under the dam are given in Table 4.5.

Table 4.4 Head along base of dam, FDIT10 and FDIT12

J=	*13*	*14*	*15*	*16*	*17*	*Remarks*
*x*m	−4	−3	−2	−1	0	
H_1(J,9)m	8.0	6.494	5.256	4.734	4.0	FDIT10 (const.k)
H_2(J,9)m	8.0	6.35	5.40	4.67	4.0	FDIT12 $k_x = 2.0$ m/day $k_y = 1.0$ m/day
H_3(J,9)m	8.0	6.35	5.58	4.766	4.0	FDIT12 $k_x = k_y = 1.0$ m/day k = 6 to 9 $k_x = k_y = 0.5$ m/day k = 1 to 5

Table 4.5 Head near centre-line under dam

K	*y*m	H_1(16,K)m	H_2(16,K)m	H_3(16,K)m
9	−0	4.73	4.67	4.77
8	−1	4.71	4.63	4.74
7	−2	4.65	4.55	4.70
6	−3	4.59	—	4.65
5	−4	4.53	—	4.59
4	−5	4.50	—	4.54
3	−6	4.47	—	4.52
2	−7	4.46	—	4.50
1	−8	4.45	—	4.50

Program FDIT12

```
100  DIM S(21,21),KX(21,21),KY(21,21)
102  INPUT "NO. COLUMNS ";J2
103  INPUT "NO. ROWS    ";K2
104  INPUT "UPSTREAM HEAD ";H1
110  INPUT "NO. ITERS";M1
111  INPUT "O/RELAX. FACTOR ";R1
114  FOR J = 1 TO J2
115 S(J,K2) = H1
116  NEXT J
117  FOR K = 1 TO K2
118 S(J2,K) = H1 / 2
119  NEXT K
130  INPUT "HORIZ. PERMEABILITY?              ";KX1
132  INPUT "VERT. PERMEABILITY? ";KY1
134  PRINT "J1,J2,K1,K2 OF KX,KY BLOCK?"
136  INPUT J3,J4,K3,K4
138  FOR J = J3 TO J4
140  FOR K = K3 TO K4
142 KX(J,K) = KX1
144 KY(J,K) = KY1
146  NEXT K: NEXT J
148  INPUT "TYPE Y FOR ANOTHER BLOCK-";A$
150  IF A$ = "Y" GOTO 130
160  INPUT "START OF DAM J=? ";J3
162 J4 = J2 - 1
180 R2 = 1.0 - R1
200  FOR M = 1 TO M1
202  PRINT "ITERATION ";M;" OF ";M1
210  FOR J = 1 TO J2
211 S(J,1) = S(J,2)
212  NEXT J
220  FOR K = 1 TO K2
221 S(1,K) = S(2,K)
222  NEXT K
230  FOR J = J3 TO J4
232 S(J,K2) = (S(J,K2 - 1) * 2 + S(J - 1,K2) + S(J + 1,K2)) / 4
234  NEXT J
250  FOR J = 2 TO J2 - 1
260  FOR K = 2 TO K2 - 1
270 S4 = S(J,K + 1) * KY(J,K)
271 S4 = S4 + S(J,K - 1) * KY(J,K - 1)
272 S4 = S4 + S(J + 1,K) * KX(J,K)
273 S4 = S4 + S(J - 1,K) * KX(J - 1,K)
274 R3 = KX(J,K) + KY(J,K) + KX(J - 1,K) + KY(J,K - 1)
275 R3 = R1 / R3
280 S(J,K) = S(J,K) * R2 + S4 * R3
290  NEXT K
300  NEXT J
```

```
310  NEXT M
320  INPUT "ROW TO BE PRINTED? ";K
325  PRINT "COL. NO.","POTENTIAL ROW ";K
326  FOR J = 1 TO J2
328  PRINT J,S(J,K)
330  NEXT J
332  INPUT "TYPE Y FOR ANOTHER ROW ";A$
334  IF A$ = "Y" GOTO 320
400  INPUT "TYPE Y FOR MORE ITERS ";A$
410  IF A$ = "Y" GOTO 200
```

Program notes

(1) Line 100 dimensions arrays S(21,21), KX(21,21) and KY(21,21). These store the head S, horizontal permeability KX and vertical permeability KY.
(2) Lines 102 to 111 input the same basic data as FDIT10. Lines 114 to 119 are also the same as FDIT10, setting the constant value boundary conditions.
(3) Lines 130 to 150 input permeability values: KX and KY values are input at lines 130 and 132. Then the J and K values defining a block of points in the grid are input in line 136. All points in this block are given the KX, KY values just input. This happens in lines 138 to 146. Another block can be dealt with if required by typing Y in response to line 148.
(4) Lines 160 to 234 are the same as the lines in FDIT10, where the iteration is set up (160 to 202) and the zero gradient boundary conditions applied (210 to 234).
(5) Lines 250 to 300 apply the finite difference equation to interior points. This is the equation given in Section 4.4.
(6) The results of the calculation are printed in the same manner as FDIT10 (lines 320 to 334).

Example 4.6 FDIT4: free surface flows – finite differences

As indicated in the previous section, free surface calculations required a solution of the Laplace equation for each adjustment of the boundary position until the condition $H = y$ is achieved on the free boundary. With finite differences this introduces at least three new features to the solution procedure and the program. First, the computation time is longer; this can be offset by compiling the program. Second, the boundary shape will not fit the edges of the grid. In the program to be used – FDIT4 – this is dealt with by storing the bottom and top points actually used in the grid at each grid column. (These are stored in the array N(21,2) set up in line

100 and used in the iteration process at line 260). This of course will only resolve the boundary shape to the nearest whole number, but the actual height of the free surface is also stored, in array Y(21). This is then used to set the boundary value of H exactly. The arrangement is illustrated in Figure 4.15, describing the problem in the example. The third new feature is the method used to adjust the surface position until the correct condition is obtained there. This can be done 'manually' by entering new surface heights Y(J), guessed at from the results of a previous solution. With seepage problems this usually works quite well and can give a solution with about five trials. With the program FDIT4 the method is to make the solution time dependent and calculate the motion of the free surface from some initial position until it approaches a steady state. The program can then be left to do the whole calculation, and it will also be useful for problems where transient behaviour is of interest. The equation for the motion of the free surface is

$$\frac{\partial y}{\partial t} = -\left(\frac{\partial H}{\partial y} - \frac{\partial H}{\partial x}\tan\alpha\right)\frac{k}{e} \tag{4.46}$$

where $\tan\alpha$ = slope of surface, $\partial y/\partial x$.
k = permeability of medium
e = porosity of medium.

A listing of FDIT4 is given below. Equation 4.46 is applied in the loop 320–340 from J = 2 to J = J2−1 through each column of the grid. The gradients $\partial H/\partial x$ and $\partial H/\partial y$ are calculated from one-sided difference formulae, $\tan\alpha$ from a central difference formula and y(J) calculated after a small increment DT. The nearest grid point to the surface is then found and the point below stored in N(J,2). The surface value of H is set to the new value of y(J).

The particular example problem is the calculation of the free surface in a rectangular porous region which holds back a head of water on the left-hand side and is open to the air on the right-hand side. Figure 4.15 shows the layout. The boundary conditions apart from the free surface are $\partial H/\partial y = 0$ on the bottom surface, implemented at line 255, H = upstream head on the left-hand face, see line 265, and $H = y$ on the right-hand face, see line 265. The data required are the number of iterations M1, relaxation factor R1, number of columns, J2, and rows, K2 in the grid, and the time interval between printing the results TP. These are read at line 110. Also read, at line 111, are the number of time steps calculated T1, the time step DT, permeability PS, porosity ES, and upstream head H1.

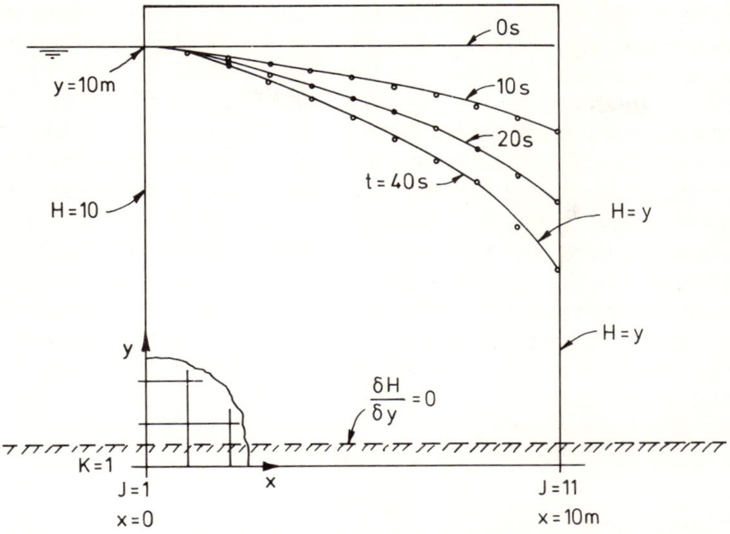

Figure 4.15 Time varying seepage calculation by finite differences

The surface profiles at various times are shown in Figure 4.15, assuming that the surface starts from a height H1 everywhere within the block. The data at lines 400 and 410 show that the number of iterations between time steps (M1) is 20, the time step DT is 1 s, the permeability PS is 0.1 m/s and porosity ES = 0.5.

Program FDIT 4

```
100 DIMENSION S(21,21),N(21,2),Y(21)
110 READ M1,R1,J2,K2,TP
111 READ T1,DT,PS,ES,H1
120 FOR J=1 TO J2
130 Y(J)=H1\N(J,2)=H1
140 FOR K=1 TO K2
150 S(J,K)=H1
151 S(0,K)=H1
160 NEXT K
170 NEXT J
180 R2=1.0-R1
190 R3=R1/4
195 FOR T=1 TO T1
200 FOR M=1 TO M1
250 FOR J=2 TO J2-1
255 S(J,1)=S(J,2)
260 FOR K=2 TO N(J,2)
265 S(1,K)=H1\S(J2,K)=K-1
270 S4=S(J,K+1)+S(J,K-1)+S(J+1,K)+S(J-1,K)
280 S(J,K)=S(J,K)*R2+S4*R3
290 NEXT K
```

```
300 NEXT J
310 NEXT M
320 FOR J=2 TO J2-1
322 K=N(J,2)
324 VS=(S(J,K)*3-S(J,K-1)*4+S(J,K-2))/2
326 US=(S(J,K)*3-S(J-1,K)*4+S(J-2,K))/2
328 TA=(Y(J+1)-Y(J-1))/2
330 Y(J)=Y(J)-(VS-US*TA)*DT*PS/ES
332 KS%=Y(J)+1.5
334 N(J,2)=KS%-1
336 S(J,KS%)=Y(J)
340 NEXT J
342 Y(J2)=Y(J2-1)*2-Y(J2-2)
345 IF T<T3 GOTO 360
346 T3=T3+TP
349 T2=T*DT
350 PRINT "SURFACE AT",T2,"SECS"
351 PRINT "Y M","X M","KS"
352 FOR J=1 TO J2
354 PRINT Y(J),J,N(J,2)
356 NEXT J
360 NEXT T
400 DATA 20,1.8,11,11,5
410 DATA 40,1,0.1,0.5,10.0
```

Program notes

(1) Line 100 dimensions arrays S(21,21) N(21,2) and Y(21). These store the values of head S on the finite difference grid, the top and bottom limits of the grid N2, N1 and the height of the free surface Y.

(2) Data are read in lines 110 and 111. M1 is the number of iterations, R1 the over-relaxation factor, J2 and K2 the number of columns and rows in the grid, and TP the time interval between printing results. T1 is the number of time steps after which the calculation stops, and DT the time step. PS and ES are the permeability and porosity of the medium. H1 is the upstream head.

(3) In lines 120 to 170 the initial values of the surface height Y (line 130) and the head S on all grid points are set equal to H1.

(4) Lines 180 and 190 calculate R2 and R3 to be used in the over-relaxation process.

(5) At line 195 the loop for each time step is started. It ends at line 360.

(6) The iteration to solve Laplace's equation occupies lines 200 to 310. Line 255 sets the vertical head gradient to zero on the base of the grid. Line 265 sets the head equal to H1 on the left-hand column of the grid and equal to the height y on the right-hand column. Lines 270 and 280 deal with internal points in the usual way. The grid is worked through column by column (line 250) and the height of each column is controlled by array N(J,2) (line 260).

(7) Lines 320 to 330 calculate the new position of the free surface after a time step. VS and US are the velocities of fluid particles at the surface. These are found from one-sided difference formulae for the

head gradient, working from the left side and from underneath the surface. TA is the slope of the surface.
(8) Lines 332 to 340 find the new height of all columns in the grid and the surface value of head at the top of these columns.
(9) Line 342 extrapolates the surface height to the right-hand boundary. This simplifies the surface slope calculation at the next column in.
(10) Lines 345 to 356 print the surface position at intervals of TP seconds. The surface height Y, column number J and column height N(J,2) are printed for each grid column.
(11) Lines 400 and 410 contain the data for that example problem.

PROBLEMS

(**4.1**) Use the boundary element program BEM2 to calculate the head on the base of the dam used in Example 4.3. If the problem is tackled by using three elements on the base of the dam (left-hand half), three on the vertical boundaries and five on the remaining top and bottom boundaries the results plotted in Figure 4.14 will be obtained. (The necessary data are at page 130.)
(**4.2**) The flow with a free surface through an embankment to a drain can be solved using the boundary element program BEM2. The boundary conditions are given in Figure 4.16 for an upstream

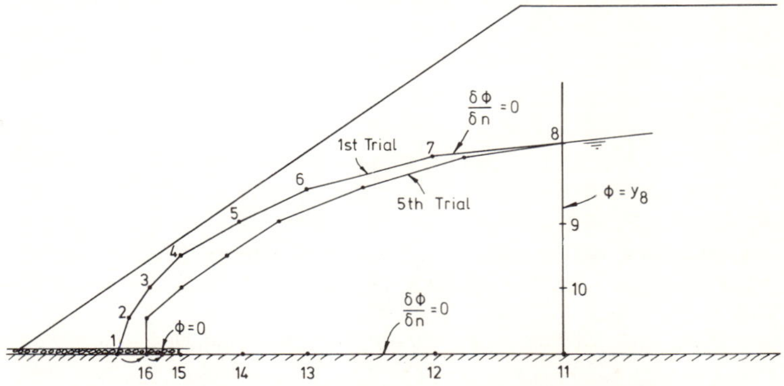

Figure 4.16 Free surface seepage to a horizontal drain by a boundary element calculation

water level of 6.5 m and the data are at page 130. The free surface position can be adjusted by running the program several times with new data for the surface points. The adjustment is carried out until the ϕ value calculated is equal to the height of the surface at the middle of an element. In this problem the x positions of the surface nodes can be changed without altering the y positions (heights) so that the target values for ϕ remain the same. After five trials the solution obtained with the mesh of Figure 4.15 was

Node	1	2	3	4	5	6	7
x	−1.0	−1.0	0	1.5	3.2	5.7	9.2
ϕ		0.53	1.38	2.38	3.39	4.31	5.33
Target ϕ		0.5	1.5	2.5	3.5	4.5	5.50

(4.3) The flow through a vertical slab can be calculated by BEM2 in a similar way to the last problem. A possible mesh for the boundary is shown in Figure 4.17, with an upstream water level of

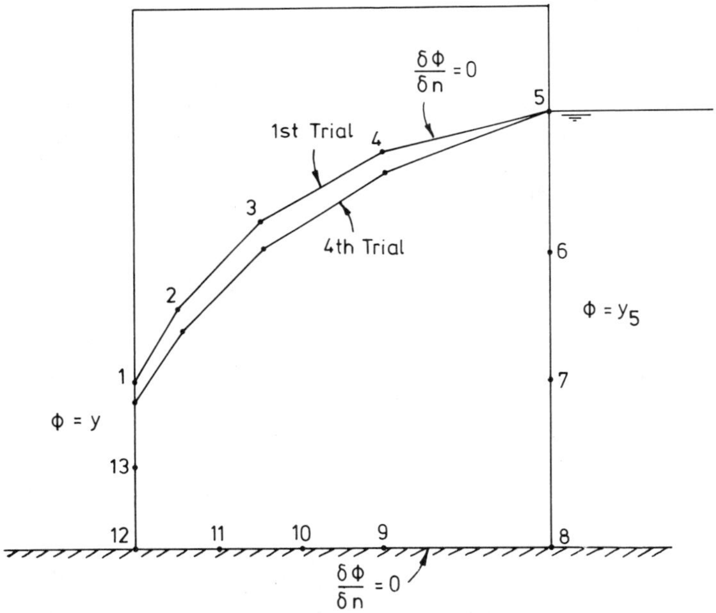

Figure 4.17 Free surface seepage in a core by a boundary element calculation

10 m and a slab thickness of 10 m. The adjustment of some surface points must be in the y direction as well as or instead of x, so a small addition to the program to calculate and print new target values for ϕ is helpful. For example, the new target value for ϕ_1 will be the average of y at node 1 and node 2. The results for surface height can be compared with the results for FDIT4 and the approximate theory of Section 4.5. Seepage flows can be calculated from the $\partial\phi/\partial n$ values at the inflow or outflow boundaries together with the lengths of the elements over which each $\partial\phi/\partial n$ value holds. The result can be

expressed as q/kh for comparison with other methods. (Necessary data are at page 131.)

(4.4) Use the finite difference method to calculate the flow under a single sheet pile and the flow into a space between two sheet piles. The outer boundary can be a rectangular while the pile or piles will be represented by vertical lines in the finite difference grid on which the stream function has a constant value. Alternatively the condition $\partial\phi/\partial n = 0$ can be imposed on these lines. This will result in a little more complicated programming. A third possibility is to represent the piles by lines of points with zero or very small horizontal permeability using the program FDIT12. The pressures and forces on the piles and the hydraulic gradients at exit from the ground can be compared with the analytical solutions from the program SPXY2.

(4.5) Use the analytical solution of program SPXY2 to calculate the seepage flow and the exit hydraulic gradient in the flow between two sheet piles shown in Figure 4.4. The width of the excavation is 6.28 m, the depth below ground level is 5.03 m and the penetration of the pile below the bottom of the hole is 2.14 m. A depth of 1.0 m of water stands above the ground outside the piles and the permeability is 0.1 m/day.

(4.6) Using the program SPXY2 or a similar program find the length of the drain required in an embankment similar to that in Figure 4.3, with an upstream water level of 12 m at a distance of 27.5 m from the end of the drain. The downstream face slopes at 1 horizontally to 1 vertically.

(4.7) Write a program to calculate the seepage quantity through the cores of rockfill dams, using the approximate theory given in the chapter. Dams without tail water can be dealt with as if the flow was horizontal in triangular cores, and in a rectangular core with tail water the Dupuit expression can be used. Calculate the seepage flow in a core with upstream and downstream slopes of 45° and an upstream water level of 10 m. Compare this with the flow through a rectangular core which is 10 m thick and retains the same head.

(4.8) Use the transient seepage program FDIT4 to calculate the steady flow through a triangular dam core and compare the results with the analytical theory for seepage rate and head on the base. The program will need to be modified slightly so that the free surface starts on the line of the downstream slope and can move below this but not above the line.

(4.9) Use the program XYSP2 to investigate the effect of a straight boundary on the drawdown of a well. Consider the effect of no flow and re-charge boundaries at distances of 100, 500, and 1000 times the well radius.

BEM2 data for the dam problem

	Remarks
700 DATA 19,4	
705 DATA (Standard gauss pts)	
710 DATA 0,0,0,3,0,6	LH boundary
720 DATA 0,8,3,8,6,8,9,8,11,8	Top boundary (Reservoir bed)
730 DATA 12,8,13,8,14,8	Dam base
740 DATA 16,8,16,6,16,3	RH boundary
750 DATA 16,0,13,0,10,0,6,0,3,0	Bottom boundary
810 DATA 100,0,100,0,100,0	ϕ, $\partial\phi/\partial n$ LH boundary
820 DATA 8,100,8,100,8,100, 8,100,8100	ϕ $\partial\phi/\partial n$ Reservoir bed
830 DATA 100,0,100,0,100,0	ϕ $\partial\phi/\partial n$ Dam base
840 DATA 0,100,0,100,0,100	ϕ $\partial\phi/\partial n$ RH boundary
850 DATA 100,0,100,0,100,0, 100,0,100,0	ϕ $\partial\phi/\partial n$ bottom

BEM2 data for free surface flow to drain

	Remarks
700 DATA 16,4	
705 DATA Standard	
710 DATA −2,0,−1.5,1.2,−1,2,0,2.8,2,4.1, 4,5,8,6	Free surface
720 DATA 12,6.5,12,4,12,2	RH boundary
730 DATA 12,0,8,0,4,0,2,0	Bottom
740 DATA 0,0,−1,0	Drain
810 DATA 100,0,100,0,100,0,100,0,100, 0,1000,0,100,0	Free surface
820 DATA 6.5,100,6.5,100,6.5,100	RH edge
830 DATA 100,0,100,0,100,0,100,0	Bottom
840 DATA 0,100,0,100	Drain

The line 710 is changed by adjusting the x values, as shown below, until $\phi = y$.

i =	1	2	3	4	5	6	7	Node number
ϕ =	0.5	1.5	2.5	3.5	4.5	5.5	6.25	Target value
ϕ_1 =	0.4	1.07	1.76	2.614	3.65	4.74	6.00	
x_2 =	−1.4	−1.4	−1.2	−0.5	1.5	3	7.5	Second trial
ϕ_2 =	0.458	1.23	1.77	2.44	3.42	4.45	5.91	
				etc.				
x_5 =	−1.0	−1.0	0	1.5	3.2	5.7	9.2	
ϕ_5 =	0.53	1.32	2.38	3.39	4.31	5.33	6.21	

BEM2 data for free surface flow through wall

	Remarks
700 DATA 13,4	
805 DATA Standard	
710 DATA 0,4,1,5.6,3,7.8,6,9.4	Free surface
720 DATA 10,10,10,7,10,4	RH edge
730 DATA 10,0,6,0,4,0,2,0	Bottom
700 DATA 0,0,0,2	LH edge
810 DATA 100,0,100,0,100,0,100,0	
820 DATA 10,100,10,100,10,100	
830 DATA 100,0,100,0,100,0,100,0	
840 DATA 1,100,3,100	

The fourth trial for the free surface gives
710 DATA 0,3.5,1,5.2,3,7.0,6,9.0
840 DATA 1,100,2.75,100

And H values on the free surface

i	=	1	2	3	4
$H_i m$	=	4.50	6.10	8.00	9.50

Chapter 5
Free surface flows

ESSENTIAL THEORY

5.1 Water surface waves

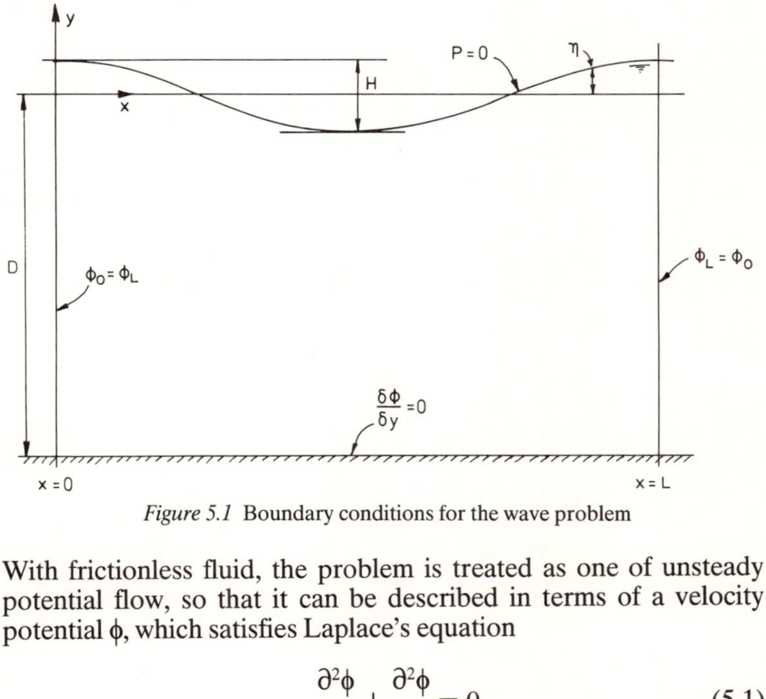

Figure 5.1 Boundary conditions for the wave problem

With frictionless fluid, the problem is treated as one of unsteady potential flow, so that it can be described in terms of a velocity potential ϕ, which satisfies Laplace's equation

$$\frac{\partial^2\phi}{\partial x^2} + \frac{\partial^2\phi}{\partial y^2} = 0 \tag{5.1}$$

The dependence on time may be dealt with by assuming that the wave is propagated in the positive direction of x with celerity c and without change of shape. The variables x and t are combined into a single variable $(x - ct)$, so that

$$\phi = \phi(x - ct, y) \tag{5.2}$$

Alternatively, by imposing a backward velocity c on the whole system, an observer will see a stationary wave, and the time-dependence is removed. The present treatment makes use of Equation 5.2.

At the bed of the channel, the vertical component of velocity $v = -\partial\phi/\partial y$ is zero. A solution which satisfies this condition, as well as Equations 5.1 and 5.2 is

$$\phi = \sum_{n=1}^{N} A_n \cosh \frac{2\pi n}{L}(D + y) \sin \frac{2\pi n}{L}(x - ct) \qquad (5.3)$$

The number of terms (N) is called the 'order' of the solution. The present treatment is confined to the first order solution, which is also called the 'linear' theory. The values of A and c are obtained as follows.

For unsteady potential flow, Bernoulli's theorem applies with a constant total energy head over the whole field. At the free surface, this becomes

$$\frac{u^2 + v^2}{2} + g\eta = \frac{\partial\phi}{\partial t} \qquad (5.4)$$

At the same time, the slope on the water surface is given by

$$\frac{d\eta}{dx} = \frac{v}{c - u} = \frac{\partial\phi/\partial y}{c - \partial\phi/\partial x} \qquad (5.5)$$

For the linear theory, which applies to waves of small amplitude, it is assumed that in Equation 5.4, the kinetic energy term is small in comparison with the other terms, and can be neglected. Also, in Equation 5.5, the horizontal component of velocity u is small in comparison with the celerity c, and is also neglected. These simplifications lead to the following results

$$A = -\frac{0.5Hc}{\sinh 2\pi D/L} \qquad (5.6)$$

$$c = \sqrt{\left(\frac{gL}{2\pi} \tanh \frac{2\pi D}{L}\right)} \qquad (5.7)$$

$$\eta = 0.5H \cos \frac{2\pi}{L}(x - ct) \qquad (5.8)$$

Period, wavelength and celerity

Equations 5.6, 5.7 and 5.8 apply when the three basic dimensions of the wave, D, L and H, are known. For many problems, the wave period T (= L/c) is known rather than the wavelength, and it is necessary to compute L and c.

In deep water, the value of tanh $2\pi D/L$ is very nearly equal to unity, so that

$$c_0 = \frac{L_0}{T} = \sqrt{\frac{gL_0}{2\pi}}, \text{ so that } L_0 = \frac{gT^2}{2\pi} \left(\text{and } c_0 = \frac{gT}{2\pi}\right) \tag{5.9}$$

the suffix 0 indicating deep water. Combining with Equation 5.7, the following expression is obtained

$$\frac{2\pi D}{L_0} = \frac{2\pi D}{L} \tanh \frac{2\pi D}{L} \tag{5.10}$$

In Equation 5.10, L is unknown. To obtain it, Equation 5.10 is inverted to give $2\pi D/L = \tanh^{-1}(L/L_0)$. The inverse tanh function is an infinite series, but it can be truncated at the second term as follows

$$\frac{2\pi D}{L} = \frac{L}{L_0} + \alpha \left(\frac{L}{L_0}\right)^3 \tag{5.11}$$

This is a quadratic equation in L^2. The value of α is found to be given by the following relationship

$$\alpha = 0.3333 + 1.0625 \frac{D}{L_0} + 5.165 \left(\frac{D}{L_0}\right)^2 \tag{5.12}$$

If D/L_0 is greater than 0.5 then $L = L_0$. L and c can be obtained when D and T are known from Equations 5.11 and 5.12. Water motions in a wave with $D/L = 1/6$ are shown in Figure 5.2.

5.2 Reflection of waves (linear theory)

When reflection is caused by a plane vertical barrier normal to the direction of propagation of the waves without dissipation of energy, the reflection is said to be perfect, and a standing wave is produced. The reflected wave has the same amplitude as the incident wave, and the following equation is obtained if $a = H/2$

$$\begin{aligned}\eta = \eta_i + \eta_r &= a \sin 2\pi(x/L - t/T) + a \sin 2\pi(x/L + t/T) \\ &= 2a \sin 2\pi x/L . \cos 2\pi t/T \end{aligned} \tag{5.13}$$

This is the equation of a standing wave.

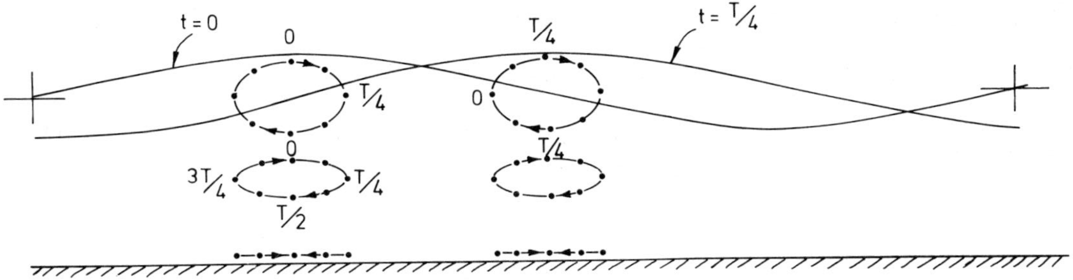

Figure 5.2 Water particle and surface positions in a progressive wave

The nodes are stationary and the amplitude of the loops increases and decreases in accordance with the cosine part of Equation 5.13. The motion of the fluid particles is obtained by compounding the orbital motions of the two systems which make up the standing waves, and it is found that the oscillatory motion of each particle is linear, being vertical at the loops, horizontal at the nodes, and inclined in between.

With an incomplete barrier, the wave is partially reflected, and partially transmitted beyond the barrier. The amplitude of the reflected wave therefore differs from that of the incident wave. Call the two amplitudes a_1 and a_2 ($a_1 > a_2$). We then get the following expression for the profile of the water surface

$$\begin{aligned}\eta &= a_1 \sin 2\pi(x/\mathrm{L} - t/T) + a_2 \sin 2\pi(x/\mathrm{L} - t/T)\\ &= (a_1 - a_2) \sin 2\pi x/\mathrm{L}.\cos \omega_2\pi t/T - (a_1 + a_2) \cos 2\pi x/\mathrm{L}.\\ &\quad \sin 2\pi t/T \qquad (5.14)\end{aligned}$$

representing a pair of standing waves out of phase superimposed on each other. The pattern is shown in Figure 5.3.

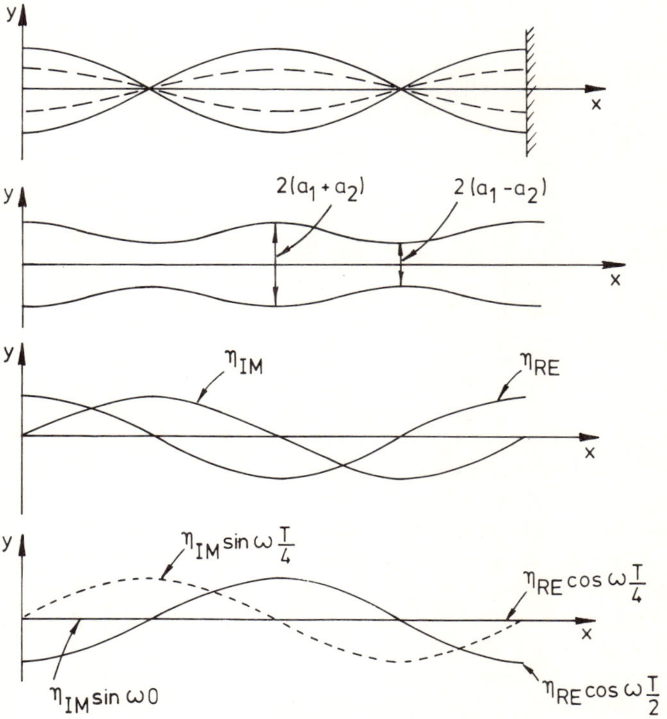

Figure 5.3 Standing waves

The positions of maximum and minimum amplitude are fixed, but there are no true nodes. The reflection coefficient is defined as

$$k_r = \frac{a_2}{a_1} = \frac{\text{max amplitude} - \text{min}}{\text{max} + \text{min}}$$

5.3 Complex potential for waves

In the previous section the standing wave was formed by adding two progressive waves moving in opposite directions. The numerical methods are more suited to calculating standing waves. A method of expressing progressive waves in terms of standing waves is required. We can see that a progressive wave can be formed by adding two standing waves which are 90° out of phase, in Figure 5.3. It is convenient to call one of the standing waves the real part of the solution (ϕ_{RE}, η_{RE}, etc.) and the other standing wave the imaginary part (ϕ_{IM}, η_{IM}, etc.). The total solution showing how ϕ varies in the x, y plane can then be written as a complex number.

$$\Phi = \phi_{RE} + \mathrm{i}\,\phi_{IM} \tag{5.15}$$

The time variation is introduced by writing

$$\begin{aligned} \phi(x,y,t) &= \text{Real part of } \phi.\mathrm{e}^{\mathrm{i}\omega t} \\ &= \phi_{RE} \cos \omega t + \phi_{IM} \sin \omega t \end{aligned} \tag{5.16}$$

with $\omega = 2\pi/T$.

5.4 The boundary element method and waves

When the boundary shapes are more complicated than a simple flat bottom, perhaps a floating object or a bottom-mounted structure, a numerical method may be needed to calculate the complex potential representing the wave. The boundary element method BEM is particularly suitable, due to the ease with which various shapes can be modelled with elements needed only on the boundary. Usually the wave is divided into two components: an incident wave, given by the progressive wave solution; and a scattered wave, to be calculated by the BEM. The sum of the two components represents the complete solution and this satisfies the zero normal flow condition on fixed impermeable portions of the boundary (e.g. fixed structures on the bed). The boundary conditions on these parts for the purpose of calculating the scattered wave is that $\partial\phi/\partial n$ scattered $= -\partial\phi/\partial n$ incident, where n = normal to boundary.

The boundary element method of Chapter 3 can be extended to deal with wave problems. As in Section 5.3, the waves are linear and described in a velocity potential which is complex. Each element thus has two unknowns, the real and imaginary parts of the potential, so the main matrices become twice as large as before. The boundary conditions are also more complex and lead to a bit more programming in the calculation of the matrix coefficient.

The boundary can be divided into four parts according to the type of boundary condition, as shown in Figure 5.4.

On (1) $\partial\phi_1/\partial n$ is given by $(-1) \times$ the incident wave $\partial\phi/\partial n$
On (2) $\partial\phi_2/\partial n = 0$
On (3) $\partial\phi_3/\partial n - \mathbf{i}m\phi_3 = 0$ (Radiation condition) $m = 2\pi/L$
On (4) $\partial\phi_4/\partial n - \omega^2/g\,\phi_4 = 0$ (Surface condition)

From the usual boundary element theory and using $\phi = V + \mathbf{i}\,W$, $\partial\phi/\partial n = R + \mathbf{i}S$ we have the matrix equation

$$\left[\begin{array}{c|c} H_1 & 0 \\ H_2 & 0 \\ H_3 & 0 \\ H_4 & 0 \\ \hline 0 & H_1 \\ & H_2 \\ 0 & H_3 \\ 0 & H_4 \end{array}\right] \times \left[\begin{array}{c} V_1 \\ V_2 \\ V_3 \\ V_4 \\ \hline W_1 \\ W_2 \\ W_3 \\ W_4 \end{array}\right] = \left[\begin{array}{c|c} G_1 & 0 \\ G_2 & 0 \\ G_3 & 0 \\ G_4 & 0 \\ \hline 0 & G_1 \\ & G_2 \\ 0 & G_3 \\ 0 & G_4 \end{array}\right] \times \left[\begin{array}{c} R^1 \\ R_2 \\ R_3 \\ R_4 \\ \hline S_1 \\ S_2 \\ S_3 \\ S_4 \end{array}\right] \qquad (5.15)$$

But from the above

R_1 is given, S_1 is given
$R_2 = 0$, $S_3 = 0$
$R_3 = m\,W_3$, $S_3 = m\,V_3$
$R_4 = +\,\omega^2/g\,V_4$, $S_4 = +\,\omega^2/g\,W_4$

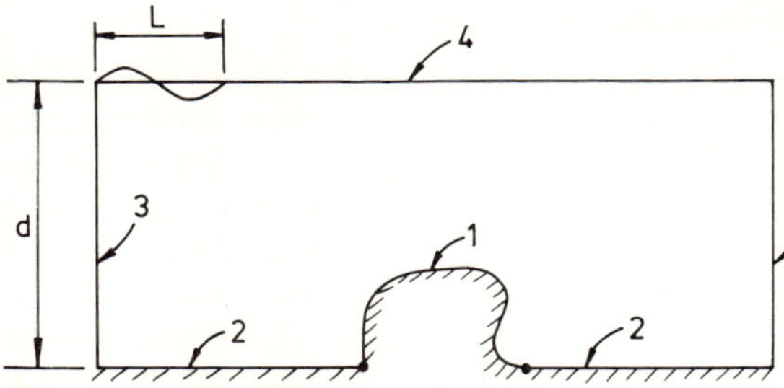

Figure 5.4 Boundary conditions for wave calculations using boundary elements

This then gives the modified equation

$$\left[\begin{array}{c|c} H_1 & 0 \\ H_2 & 0 \\ H_3 & mG_3 \\ H_4 - \omega^2 g G_4 & 0 \\ \hline 0 & H_1 \\ 0 & H_2 \\ -mG_3 & H_3 \\ 0 & H_4 - \omega^2 g \end{array}\right] \times \left[\begin{array}{c} V_1 \\ V_2 \\ V_3 \\ V_4 \\ \hline W_1 \\ W_2 \\ W_3 \\ W_4 \end{array}\right] = \left[\begin{array}{c|c} G_1 & 0 \\ 0 & 0 \\ 0 & 0 \\ 0 & 0 \\ \hline 0 & G_1 \\ 0 & 0 \\ 0 & 0 \\ 0 & 0 \end{array}\right] \times \left[\begin{array}{c} R_1 \\ 0 \\ 0 \\ 0 \\ \hline S_1 \\ 0 \\ 0 \\ 0 \end{array}\right] \quad (5.16)$$

in which the unknowns are all on the LHS. For programming it is convenient to write this as

$$\left[\begin{array}{c|c} H_1 + C_1 G_1 & D_1 G_1 \\ H_2 + C_2 G_2 & D_2 G_2 \\ H_3 + C_3 G_3 & D_3 G_3 \\ H_4 + C_4 G_4 & D_4 G_4 \\ \hline -D_1 G_1 & H_1 + C_1 G_1 \\ -D_2 G_2 & H_2 + C_2 G_2 \\ -D_3 G_3 & H_3 + C_3 G_3 \\ -D_4 G_4 & H_4 + C_4 G_4 \end{array}\right] \times \left[\begin{array}{c} V_1 \\ V_2 \\ V_3 \\ V_4 \\ \hline W_1 \\ W_2 \\ W_3 \\ W_4 \end{array}\right] = \left[\begin{array}{c|c} E_1 G_1 & 0 \\ E_2 G_2 & 0 \\ E_3 G_3 & 0 \\ E_4 G_4 & 0 \\ \hline 0 & E_1 G_1 \\ 0 & E_2 G_2 \\ 0 & E_3 G_3 \\ 0 & E_4 G_4 \end{array}\right] \times \left[\begin{array}{c} R_1 \\ 0 \\ 0 \\ 0 \\ \hline S_1 \\ 0 \\ 0 \\ 0 \end{array}\right] \quad (5.17)$$

with $C_1 = C_2 = C_3 = 0,\ C_4 = \omega^2/g$
$D_1 = D_2 = D_4 = 0,\ D_3 = m$
$E_2 = E_3 = E_4 = 0,\ E_1 = 1$

5.5 Reflected and transmitted waves

The scattered wave solution from the BEM program provides the reflected wave on the front side of the obstacle and the transmitted wave is found by adding the scattered wave and incident wave on the rear side. The total wave solution is of course the sum of the incident wave and the scattered wave, but it is useful to split it into incident, reflected and transmitted components to compare the effect of various barriers and obstacles on a wave. This information is usually expressed as reflection and transmission coefficients K_r and K_t

$$K_r = \frac{H_r}{H_i}, \quad K_t = \frac{H_t}{H_i} \tag{5.18}$$

where H_i = incident wave height
H_r = reflected wave height
H_t = transmitted wave height.

If there is no energy lost at the barrier, as will be the case for a

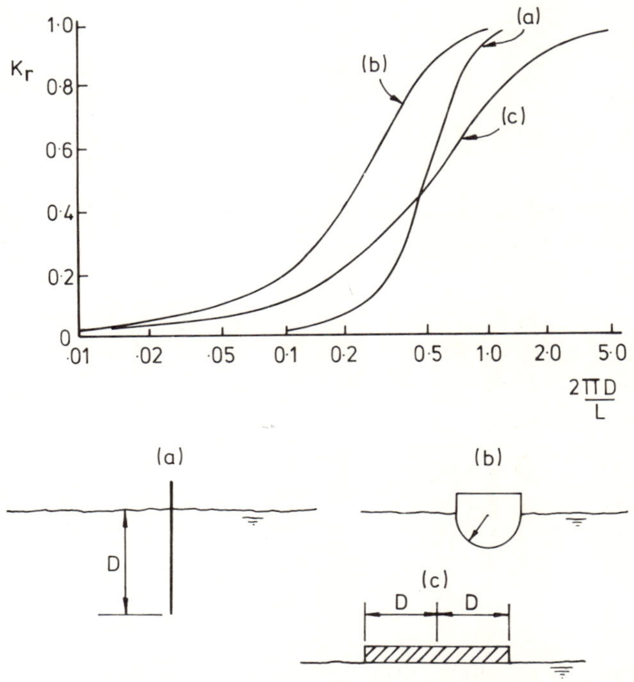

Figure 5.5 Wave reflection from various shapes (after Ippen, *Estuary and Pipeline Hydrodynamics*, McGraw-Hill, 1966, with permission)

fixed obstacle in ideal flow, then using the fact that wave energy flux is proportional to H^2

$$\begin{aligned} H^2_t &= H^2_i - H^2_r \\ K^2_t &= 1 - K^2_r \end{aligned} \tag{5.19}$$

Some results for simple fixed shapes are shown in Figure 5.5. These are a vertical plate, a horizontal plate on the surface and a semicircular shape, all in deep water. We can see that the results depend on the ratio of the size of the obstacle to the length of the wave. For the vertical plate, when $D = L/2\pi$, K_r is nearly equal to 1 and practically all the wave energy is reflected. For a longer plate or shorter waves, the waves will be completely reflected. For a shorter plate or longer waves more wave energy gets past the obstacle, and at $D = (L/2\pi)\,0.5$, K_r is about 0.6, $K_t \simeq 0.8$. An approximate theory, which fits the results for the vertical plate quite well, is that the energy in the wave above the bottom of the plate is reflected and the energy below is transmitted. That is

$$E_r = \int_{-D}^{0} \frac{\partial \phi}{\partial x} \cdot \frac{\partial \phi}{\partial t}\, dy$$

i.e. in deep water

$$E_r = \text{Const.} \int_{-D}^{0} \left(\exp \frac{2\pi}{L} y \right)^2 dy$$

$$E_i = \text{Const.} \int_{-L/2}^{0} \left(\exp \frac{2\pi}{L} y \right)^2 dy$$

$$= \text{Const.} \left[\frac{L}{4\pi} \exp \frac{4\pi}{L} y \right]_{L/2}^{0}$$

$$K^2_r = \frac{H^2_r}{H^2_i} = \frac{E_r}{E_i} = \frac{\left[\exp \frac{4\pi}{L} y \right]_{-D}^{0}}{\left[\exp \frac{4\pi}{L} y \right]_{-L/2}^{0}}$$

$$K_r = \frac{H_r}{H_i} = \left[\frac{\exp 0 - \exp \dfrac{-4\pi}{L} D}{\exp 0 - \exp \dfrac{-4\pi}{L} L/2}\right]^{1/2}$$

$$= \left[\frac{1 - \exp \dfrac{-4\pi}{L} D}{1 - \exp -2\pi}\right]^{1/2}$$

$$= \left[1 - \exp \frac{-4\pi D}{L}\right]^{1/2} \tag{5.20}$$

The semicircular shape is effective over a greater range of D/L, starting to reflect energy at smaller values of D/L than the vertical plate and giving total reflection at a slightly smaller D/L. The horizontal plate is also effective over a wider range of D/L but does not give total reflection until higher D/L than the vertical plate.

The submerged circular cylinder is an interesting case. This shape does not reflect waves but merely changes the phase of the wave as it passes over.

5.6 Forces on large 2D objects fixed in waves

The forces on an object in a wave, like the reflection of waves, depend on the ratio of the size of the object D (its length or depth, say) to the wave length of the wave L. Also important is the ratio of the water particle orbit A (its radius, say) to the size of the object. Small values of A/D are bound to arise when D/L is large, since A/L must be small for linear waves. In this case the pressure can be calculated from the $\partial\phi/\partial t$ term in Bernoulli's equation alone, and forces follow from the pressure.

The forces on a large vertical plate can therefore be found by integrating $-\rho\ \partial\phi/\partial t$ from the water surface to the bottom of the plate, using the ϕ expression for a standing wave; i.e.

$$F_x = \int_{-D}^{0} -\rho \frac{\partial \phi}{\partial t}\, dy \tag{5.21}$$

with

$$\phi = -\frac{H}{2} \frac{c}{\sinh \dfrac{2\pi d}{L}} \cosh\left(\frac{d+y}{L}\right) \sin 2\pi \left(\frac{x}{L} - \frac{t}{T}\right)$$

or in deep water

$$\phi = \frac{-Hc}{2} \exp \frac{2\pi y}{L} \sin 2\pi \left(\frac{x}{t} - \frac{t}{T}\right)$$

$$\frac{\partial \phi}{\partial t} = -\frac{\pi}{T} HC \exp \frac{2\pi y}{L} \cos 2\pi \left(\frac{x}{L} - \frac{t}{T}\right)$$

The horizontal and vertical forces on a half cylinder on the sea bed with a depth to radius $d/a = 3.0$ were calculated by Chakrabati. The results are expressed as $f = \text{force}/\rho g\, H/2\, a$ as a function of $2\pi a/L$, in the table below

$\frac{2\pi a}{L}$	0.1	0.2	0.4	0.6	1.0
f_x	0.3	0.533	0.687	0.6	0.3
f_y	1.89	1.69	1.17	0.61	0.28

5.7 Wave forces on vertical cylinders

A more common structural element is the vertical circular cylinder, shown in Figure 5.6. Here the wave can be assumed to pass unchanged if the value of D/L is less than 1/5. The force on a short length of the cylinder can then be found in terms of the velocity and acceleration that would occur in a wave at the position of the centre of the cylinder (in the cylinder's absence). If A/D is less than about 1, there will be no vortices generated by separation of the flow and potential flow results for the force will hold, so

$$F_x = \frac{\pi D^2}{4} \rho\, C_M \frac{\partial u}{\partial t} \Delta y$$

If A/D is very large, on the other hand, because the wave is large or the cylinder small, then the flow is more like a steady flow with separation and the force is given by

$$F_x = D\, 1/2 \rho\, u^2\, C_D\, \Delta y$$

In fact the parameter used to determine the type of force, inertia or drag or a combination of the two is the Keulegan–Carpenter number, $KC = U_{max} T/D$ (i.e. $2\pi\, A/D$). The expression for force is the Morison equation

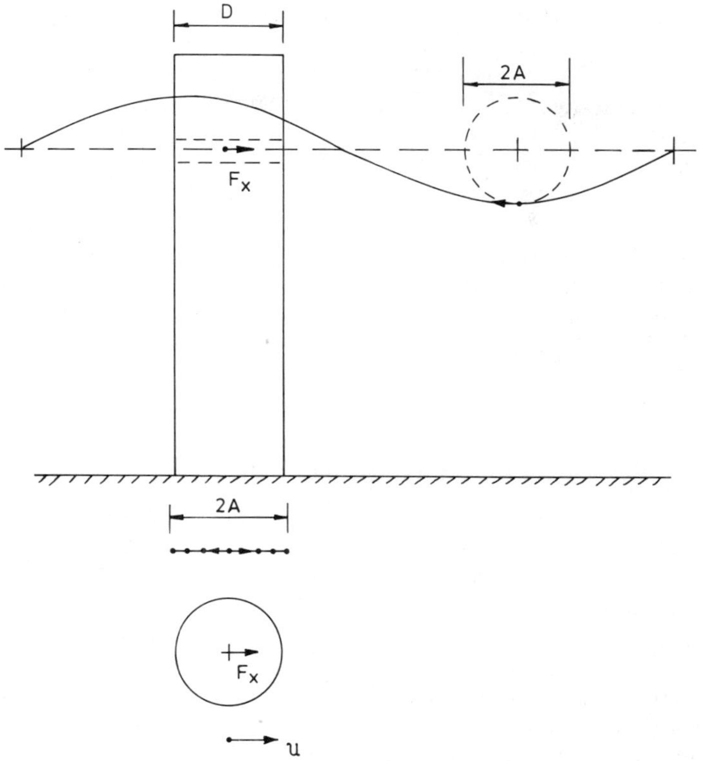

Figure 5.6 Water motion near a vertical cylinder in a progressive wave

$$F_x = 1/2\,\rho\,u^2\,C_D\,D\,\Delta y$$

$$+\rho\,\frac{\partial\phi}{\partial t}\;C_M\;\frac{\pi D^2}{4}\,\Delta y \qquad (5.23)$$

The values of drag coefficient C_D and inertia coefficient C_M vary with KC and with the Reynolds number RE = $U_{max}\ D/\nu$. Also important is the relative roughness of the cylinder surface. The effects of Re and k/D on the drag coefficient C_D are of a similar nature to their effects in steady flow, so a sub-critical and post-critical behaviour can be identified at low (Re $< 8 \times 10^4$) intermediate (Re $\simeq 10^4 - 6 \times 10^5$) and high Reynolds numbers. At high KC values where the flow is more like a steady flow, C_D is slightly larger than the steady flow value. It increases to about 1.7 times the steady flow value at KC = 10 before reducing as the separation region becomes smaller. The inertia coefficient has a potential flow value of $C_M = 2.0$, and for low KC, C_M tends towards this value. The value tends towards a minimum at KC $\simeq$ 15 and tends to a value of about C_M = 1.0 for a subcritical flow with a relatively high C_D and large wake. In a critical flow for a smooth cylinder with a low C_D and a small wake, the flow pattern is more like the potential flow and C_M has a higher value, around 1.7. Extensive data on these coefficients can be found in the bibliography at Section 5.14.

Some examples of average values from full-scale tests are:

Test	KC	C_D	C_M	Re
(a)	—	0.9	1.7	—
(b)	17–24	0.8	1.5	$\sim 4.5 \times 10^5$
(c)	15–35	0.6	1.21	$2\text{–}8 \times 10^5$

5.8 Wave forces on large vertical cylinders

When the cylinder diameter is greater than about one-fifth of the wave length, the wave is affected by the presence of the cylinder and the forces can be calculated by the use of diffraction theory. The BEM and FEM are often used to do this but it will not be covered in the present work. However, once the results are known they can be expressed as an inertia coefficient C_M which is used in the same way as in Morison's equation; that is, the force on a short length of cylinder is

$$F_x = \rho \frac{\pi D^2}{4} C_M \Delta y \frac{\partial u}{\partial t}$$

C_M now varies with the ratio of diameter to wave length D/L. At small D/L C_M is still approximately 2.0 but as the cylinder increases in size relative to the wave length C_M reduces as shown in the table below. The phase of the force also changes and this is shown by the results for phase angle δ as a function of D/L:

$\frac{D}{L}$	0	0.2	0.4	0.6	0.8	1.0	1.2	1.4
f_A	—	0.6	1.35	1.5	1.98	2.22	2.44	2.64
$\delta°$	0	15	19	−2	−30	−64	−95	−130

$$C_M = f_A / \left[\left(\frac{D}{L} \right)^2 \frac{\pi^3}{4} \right]$$

$\delta°$ = phase lag in degrees

5.9 Other free surface flows

The previous sections have dealt with flows caused by fluctuations of the free surface about a mean position. These fluctuations (i.e. wave heights) have been small enough to allow the boundary conditions to be applied at the mean position and applied in a form which neglects the U^2 terms in Bernoulli's equation . We now turn to some flows where the free surface is steady in position but varies considerably in height from one part of the flow to another and so the (velocity)^2 terms must be included in the boundary condition. The position of the free surface is also unknown at the start of the calculation and must be determined as the problem is solved. Typical flows of this sort are the flows under sluices and gates in open channels, and the flow over weirs and spillways of various shapes.

5.10 The x–ψ coordinate system

To deal with free surface problems of the sort just mentioned it is convenient sometimes to work in a new coordinate system. Instead of finding ψ or ϕ at fixed points in the x, y plane we can find the height y of streamlines ($\psi =$ const.) at fixed x values. The coordinate system is now (x,ψ) and the variable to be found is y. The main advantage of this is that the mechanism for changing the surface height is included in any program to solve the problem, and the grid or mesh system does not need to be redefined when the surface shape is adjusted. A simple finite difference procedure using a regular grid on a rectangular region can be used to solve the equation for y, and yet quite complex surface shapes can still be modelled. An example of such a grid used to model flow from a nozzle is shown in Figure 5.11. The equation for y in this system is more complicated than the Laplace equation; it is now

$$\frac{\partial^2 y}{\partial x^2}\left(\frac{\partial y}{\partial \psi}\right)^2 + \frac{\partial^2 y}{\partial \psi^2}\left[1+\left(\frac{\partial y}{\partial x}\right)^2\right] - 2\frac{\partial^2 y}{\partial x \partial \psi}\frac{\partial y}{\partial x}\frac{\partial y}{\partial \psi} = 0 \qquad (5.24)$$

This can be solved by a relaxation method in a similar way to the Laplace equation. The finite difference expression for y at a grid point now involves eight surrounding points instead of four, however. The boundary conditions are input as heights of the steamlines of the flow at the top, bottom and ends. Usually the height of the bottom streamline is known (e.g. if it represents the bed of a channel), and at the ends the velocity may be uniform, giving an equal spacing of the streamlines. The top streamline is often the free surface and this must be adjusted until the following condition is met

$$\frac{p}{\rho g} = B_0 - \left(\frac{u^2 + v^2}{2g}\right) - y_s = 0 \qquad (5.25)$$

where B_0 = Bernoulli constant = $p_0/\rho g + (U^2{}_0 + V^2{}_0)/2g + y$
= Total head.

Velocities are calculated from the relationships

$$u = \frac{\partial \psi}{\partial y} = \frac{1}{(\Delta y/\Delta \psi)} \qquad (5.26)$$

$$v = u\,\frac{\Delta y}{\Delta x} \qquad (5.27)$$

The simplest way of adjusting the free surface is 'manually' to enter a new estimate of the surface ys once the pressure on the surface, or the total head, has been calculated for the previous estimated surface. The new estimate is made in such a way as to try to satisfy the surface condition on the pressure. It should be possible to include this process in the program. Reference 5.1 (see Section 5.14) suggests that the automatic adjustment of surface height is a sensitive procedure, in particular for flows like the weir flow where a 'zone of uncertainty' exists around the critical flow region, near the weir crest. The reference suggests a Newton-Raphson technique be used to calculate the corrections to y given by

$$(\Delta y) = \left[\frac{\mathrm{d}B}{\mathrm{d}y}\right]^{-1}(\Delta B) \qquad (5.28)$$

where (Δy) is the vector of y corrections and (ΔB) is the vector of total head errors for the surface points. The matrix $[\mathrm{d}B/\mathrm{d}y]$ must be calculated by adjusting each surface point independently and calculating ΔB at every point caused by this adjustment. In Reference 5.2. a shorter adjustment procedure was sufficient for a sluice gate problem; here the formula used is equivalent to

$$\Delta y^{k+1}{}_i = \frac{\Delta B^k{}_i\, W}{\dfrac{\Delta B^k{}_i - \Delta B_i^{k-1}}{\Delta y^k{}_i}} \qquad (5.29)$$

where Δy^k_i = y correction for point i at kth trial
$\Delta B^k{}_i$ = Error in total head at point i at kth trial
W = Relaxation factor.

Whatever method is used, some limits on the correction to y should be employed to ensure that the depth of flow stays within reasonable limits and a suitable curve is obtained for the surface.

5.11 Flows from an orifice

The flow through a two-dimensional orifice can be solved by the classical methods of mapping so long as the pressure equation on the free surface reduces to the requirement that $u^2 + v^2 = \text{constant}$, i.e. the velocity along the free surface is constant. This condition will be met if the flow from the orifice is relatively fast so that gravity has a small effect on the flow. The important quantity that can be calculated is the contraction coefficient C_C, giving the ratio of the final jet width to the width of the orifice opening. C_C varies with the upstream width of the flow B and the angle of edge of the orifice β, defined in Figure 5.7. The results in Table 5.1 were obtained by Von Mises for C_C.

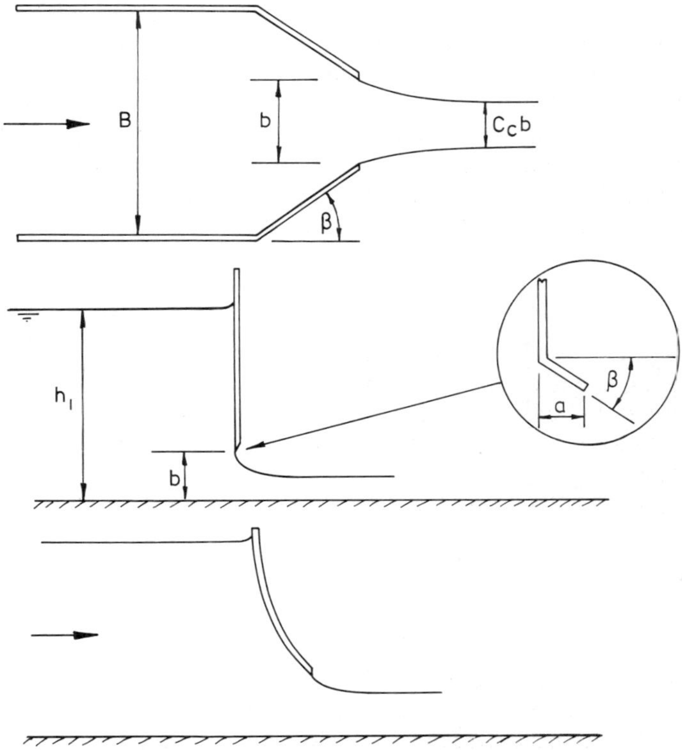

Figure 5.7 Free surface flow from orifices and gates

Table 5.1 Results for C_C obtained by Von Mises

$\frac{b}{B}$	$\beta = 45°$	$\beta = 90°$	$\beta = 135°$	$\beta = 180°$
0	0.746	0.611	0.537	0.500
0.1	0.747	0.612	0.546	0.513
0.2	0.747	0.616	0.555	0.528
0.4	0.749	0.631	0.580	0.564
0.6	0.758	0.662	0.620	0.613
0.8	0.789	0.722	0.698	0.691
1.0	1.0	1.0	1.0	1.0

The coefficient of discharge C_d from the opening can be defined by

$$q = C_d \, b \sqrt{\frac{2\Delta p}{\rho}} \tag{5.31}$$

hence

$$C_d = \frac{C_c}{\sqrt{\left[1 - C_C^2 \left(\frac{b}{B}\right)^2\right]}}$$

It can be found that the values of C_C for the 2D case given above are a good approximation to the ratio of the jet and orifice areas in a circular orifice flow (with b/B replaced by d/D).

5.12 Sluice gates

The flow under various types of control gate in an open channel cannot be easily calculated by the classical methods because gravity has an important effect on the flow and the full expression for pressure (Equation 5.25) must be applied on the free surface. Two common types of sluice gate are sketched in Figure 5.7: the vertical sluice gate; and a sluice gate forming an arc of a circle, called a Tainter gate.

For the vertical sluice gate the coefficient of contraction C_C varies much less with the upstream flow geometry, b/h_1, than for the orifice. In fact C_C is between 0.605 and 0.61 for b/h_1 from 0 to 0.5. The flow can be calculated from

$$q = C_d\, b \sqrt{2gh_1} \tag{5.32}$$

with

$$C_d = \frac{C_C}{\sqrt{-(C_c\, b/h_1)^2}}$$

If the bottom edge of the gate is bevelled or distorted in some other way, the contraction and discharge coefficients may be affected considerably. Ligget *et al.*, Reference 5.1, calculated the effect of a small bevelled tip as shown in Figure 5.7. For the case $b/h_1 = 0.3$ and $a/h_1 = 0.003$ the following results were found, for various bevel angles, β:

β	C_C	C_d
90°	0.600	0.550
45°	0.630	0.576
14.5°	0.652	0.597
0°	0.692	0.630

The downstream water level will affect the discharge if the free jet is drowned. An approximate theory would give the submerged jet a C_C of 0.61 and a hydrostatic pressure equal to that of the downstream water level. Then

$$q = v_1\, h_1 = v_2 C_C b$$

$$h_1 + \frac{v^2{}_1}{2g} = h_2 + \frac{v^2{}_2}{2g}$$

$$q = v_2\, C_C\, b = \left[2g \frac{(h_1 - h_2)}{1 - C^2{}_C \left(\dfrac{b}{h_1} \right)^2} \right]^{1/2} C_C\, b$$

$$C_d = \left[2g \frac{(h_1 - h_2)}{1 - C^2{}_C \left(\dfrac{b}{h_1} \right)^2} \right]^{1/2} \frac{C_C\, b}{\sqrt{(2g\, h_1\, b)}}$$

$$C_d = \left[\frac{1 - \left(\frac{h_2}{h_1} \right)}{1 - \left(C_C \frac{b}{h_1} \right)^2} \right]^{1/2} C_C \tag{5.33}$$

The discharge coefficient for the Tainter gate depends on the relative height of the pivot d/R, the relative gap of the opening b/R upstream geometry h_1/R, and the downstream depth if the outflow is drowned. For the free discharge case some typical values of C_d are given in Table 5.2.

Table 5.2 Some typical values of C_d for the free discharge case

d/R	b/R	h_1/R	C_d
0.1	0.1	1.0	0.57
0.1	0.3	1.0	0.53
0.1	0.5	1.0	0.500
0.5	0.1	1.0	0.62
0.5	0.3	1.0	0.55
0.5	0.5	1.0	0.52
0.9	0.1	1.0	0.73
0.9	0.3	1.0	0.61
0.9	0.5	1.0	0.54

Gates may also be of the overflow type and these will be mentioned after the section on weirs which follows.

5.13 Weirs and spillways

The basic flow over a sharp crested weir with a ventilated nappe is sketched in Figure 5.8. Here we have an upper and also a lower free surface on which the pressure is atmospheric (taken as zero for convenience). The discharge per unit width is given by

$$q = C_d H^{3/2} r \frac{2}{3} \sqrt{2g} \tag{5.34}$$

with

$$C_d = 0.611 + 0.075 \frac{H}{h}$$

The shape of the lower nappe is of interest since a weir of this shape should have zero pressure on its surface at the design head. It is

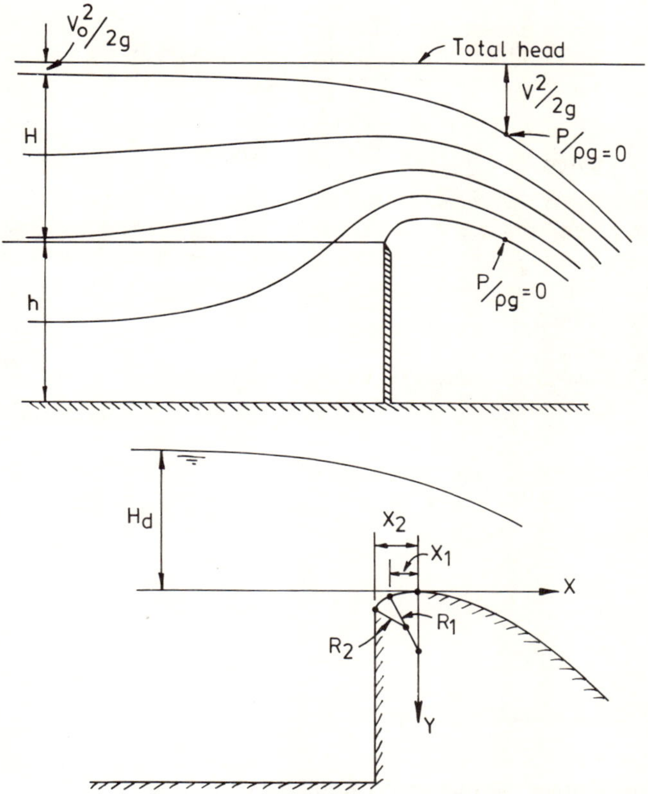

Figure 5.8 Flow over weirs

important when designing large spillways to ensure that the pressure does not fall too low and cause cavitation, with subsequent damage to the spillway surface. A standard set of spillway profiles which approximate to the shape of the lower nappe have been developed, see Chow. They follow the equation

$$X^n = K\,H_d^{n-1}\ Y \tag{5.35}$$

where X and Y are defined in Figure 5.8, H_d is the design head, and K and n are constants given below;

Slope of upstream face	K	n
Vertical	2.0	1.85
3 on 1	1.936	1.836
3 on 2	1.939	1.810
3 on 3	1.873	1.776

The curves upstream of the origin for X and Y, which is the highest point on the weir, are circles with radii given by

Slope	$\frac{R_1}{H_d}$	$\frac{R_2}{H_d}$	$\frac{X_1}{H_d}$	$\frac{X_2}{H_d}$
Vertical	0.5	0.2	0.175	0.282
3 on 1	0.68	0.21	0.139	0.273
3 on 3	0.45	—	0.119	—

The discharge per unit width is given by

$$q = C_d H^{3/2} \tag{5.36}$$

with $C_d = 2.226\,\text{m}^2/\text{s}$ for $h/H > 1.33$. With this condition the approach velocity is negligible.

For heads other than the design head, the coefficient of discharge C may be found from a plot of H/H_d versus C/C_d, which gives the values in the table below

$\frac{H_1}{H_d}$	1.4	1.2	1.0	0.8	0.6	0.4	0.2
$\frac{C}{C_d}$	1.04	1.025	1.0	0.975	0.945	0.9	0.82

H_d now includes the velocity head $v^2_0/2g$.

The water surface profile for a spillway with a vertical upstream face and no piers can be found from Table 5.3 for three operating heads. The pressures on the spillway surface are also given.

Another type of weir, which is widely used for flow measurement, is the crump weir. This has a triangular profile in the stream direction, with an upstream slope of 2 horizontal to 1 vertical and a downstream slope of 5 horizontal to 1 vertical, as shown in Figure 5.12. The equation for the discharge per unit width is

$$q = 0.628\sqrt{g}(H - 0.003)^{3/2} \tag{5.37}$$

(The ideal flow near the crest will in fact have a curved boundary since a separation bubble forms at the sharp crest which will form a constant pressure boundary. The shape is given in Reference 5.3 as a circular arc.)

The drum gate is an overflow gate acting like a movable weir, which is sometimes fitted at the top of a spillway. The gate surface is a circular arc of radius R, pivoted at the bottom edge of the arc. The

Table 5.3

	$H/H_d = 0.5$		$H/H_d = 1.0$		$H/H_d = 1.33$	
$\frac{X}{H_d}$	$\frac{Y}{H_d}$	$\frac{H_p}{H_d}$	$\frac{Y}{H_d}$	$\frac{H_p}{H_d}$	$\frac{Y}{H_d}$	$\frac{H_p}{H_d}$
−1.0	−0.490	—	−0.933	—	−1.21	—
−0.8	−0.484	—	−0.915	—	−1.185	—
−0.6	−0.475	—	−0.893	—	−1.151	—
−0.4	−0.460	+	−0.865	+	−1.11	+
−0.2	−0.425	+0.32	−0.821	+0.02*	−1.06	−0.47**
0	−0.371	+0.20	−0.755	+0.0*	−1.0	−0.35**
0.2	−0.300	+0.17	−0.681	+0.06	−0.91	−0.19
0.4	−0.200	+0.12	−0.586	+0.02	−0.821	−0.18
0.6	−0.075	+0.10	−0.465	+0.03	−0.705	−0.13
0.8	−0.075	+0.08	−0.320	+0.04	−0.569	−0.07
1.0	0.258	—	−0.145	—	−0.411	+
1.2	0.470	—	0.055	—	−0.220	—
1.4	0.705	—	0.294	—	−0.002	—
1.6	0.972	—	0.563	—	0.243	—
1.8	1.269	—	0.857	—	0.531	—

*Min $H_p/H_d = -0.0$ at $X/H_d = -0.18$

**Min $H_p/H_d = -0.48$ at $X/H_d = -0.18$

discharge depends on the angle between the downstream gate lip and the horizontal θ. For an angle of $\theta = 30°$ the discharge coefficient C_d becomes independent of H/R.

$$q = C_d H^{3/2} \qquad C_d = 2.143 \tag{5.38}$$

For other values of θ, C_d varies with H/R, see Chow.

5.14 Bibliography

1. Chow, V. T., *Open channel hydraulics,* McGraw-Hill (1959).
2. Weigel, R. L., *Oceanographical engineering,* Prentice Hall (1964).
3. Zienkiewicz, O. C., *et al. Numerical methods in offshore engineering,* Wiley (1978)
4. Shaw, T. L. (Ed), *Mechanics of wave induced forces on cylinders,* Pitman (1979)
5. Birkhoff, G. and Zarantonello, E. M., *Jets, wakes and cavities,* Academic Press (1957).

References

5.1 Cheng, Ligget, Lui, *Proc. ASCE Hyd. Div.*, Vol. 107, HY10, Oct. 1981, p. 1163–78.
5.2 Masliyah, J. H. *et. al., ASCE HY*, June 1985.
5.3 Smith, K. V. (Ed), *Channel Control Structures*, Springer Verlag.

WORKED EXAMPLES

Example 5.1 WAVE1: wave length and celerity

A program to calculate the wave length L and clerity C of a wave, given its period T and the water depth D, is given below. It avoids trial solutions for the tanh $2\pi D/L$ expression by using Equations 5.11 and 5.12, which can be evaluated directly. The program can be checked on the example of a wave with period $T = 8.003$ secs in water of depth $D = 10$ m. (This wave has a deepwater wave length $L_0 = 100$ m.) The program gives $L = 70.9706$ m and $C = 8.868$ m/s. Equation 5.7 allows the value of C to be checked, from

$$C = \left(\frac{gL}{2\pi}\tanh\frac{2\pi D}{L}\right)^{1/2}$$

$$C = 8.864\,\text{m/s}$$

The program is written for a programmable pocket calculator.

Program WAVE1

```
10   SET F 4
20   INPUT"D= ",D
30   INPUT"T= ",T
40   K=9.81*T^2/(2*PI)
45   PRINT"L0= ",K
50   X=D/K
60   A=1/3+1.0625*X+5.165*X^2
70   IF X>0.5; Y=1
80   IF X<0.5; Y=SQR(SQR(.25/A^2+2*PI*X/4)-.5/A)
90   L=K*Y
100  C=L/T
110  PRINT"L= ",L
120  PRINT"C= ",C
130  END
```

Program notes

(1) Line 10 gives 4 decimal places on the particular calculator used. This could be omitted on most micros.
(2) Lines 20 and 30 input the water depth D and wave period T.

(3) Line 40 calculates the deepwater length and denotes this by K since the calculator used employs only single letters for variables. Note there is a symbol for π. Normally the symbol L_0 is used and L_0 (= K) can be printed by line 45 if this line is included.
(4) Line 50 calculates X = Depth/Deepwater wave length. This is then used in Equation 5.12 at line 60.
(5) Line 70 calculates L/L_0, denoted by Y for the deepwater case, $D/L_0 > 0.5$.
(6) Line 80 finds L/L_0 for the intermediate and shallow depths by solving a quadratic equation.
(7) Lines 90 and 100 calculate wave length L and celerity C. These are printed in lines 110 and 120.

Example 5.2 WAVE2: surface and water movement in waves

The program listed below is written to plot the surface profile and positions of particles moving with the water in a wave. The surface profile can be plotted at selected times in the wave period. A few profiles will reveal how the wave is moving while many profiles will show the wave envelope; that is, the limits within which the surface moves. After the surface has been plotted, the positions of a number of water particles can be plotted again at selected times in the wave period. As an example, typical results for a progressive wave of length $L = 24$ m in depth $D = 4$ m are shown in Figure 5.2. The wave height is 2 m. A feature of the program is that it uses the idea of a real part and an imaginary part of the wave solution and shows the result of combining the two. In keeping with this philosophy the user is asked to input a real wave height and an imaginary wave height. (If these are numerically equal a progressive wave results, if one is zero a standing wave is formed.) The data to produce a plot similar to Figure 5.2 is shown below after the program. The plot is produced on a screen measuring 360 units horizontally by 160 units vertically and one wave length of the surface is plotted; hence the need to scale the x and y coordinates and offset the origin which has y zero on the still water level.

Program WAVE2

```
100  DIM S(100),X(100),Y(100)
150  INPUT "WAVE HT. REAL ";H1
160  INPUT "WAVE HT. IMAG. ";H2
170  INPUT "WATER DEPTH ";D
180  INPUT "WAVE LENGTH ";L
200  GOSUB 1000: REM   SETS UP PLO              T
```

```
210  INPUT "NO. OF SURFACE PTS. ";J1
250  INPUT "TIME/PERIOD ";T1
260  GOSUB 1100: REM  PLOTS SURFACE
270  INPUT "ANOTHER PLOT?(Y/N) ";A$
280  IF A$ = "Y" GOTO 250
300  HGR : HOME : HCOLOR= 3
305  VTAB 24
310  INPUT "NO. OF TRACER PTS. ";J2
320  FOR J = 1 TO J2
330  INPUT "X POSN.   ";X(J)
332  INPUT "Y POSN.   ";Y(J)
340  NEXT J
350  INPUT "TIME/PERIOD ";T1
360  GOSUB 2000: REM  PLOTS TRACER POSN.
370  INPUT "ANOTHER PLOT?(Y/N) ";A$
380  IF A$ = "Y" GOTO 350
400  STOP
1000  REM  SETS UP PLOT
1010  INPUT "SCALE FACTOR X ";SX
1020  INPUT "SCALE FACTOR Y ";SY
1030  INPUT "X OFFSET ";XS
1040  INPUT "Y OFFSET ";YS
1060  HOME : HGR
1070  HCOLOR= 3: VTAB 24
1080  RETURN
1100  REM  PLOTS SURFACE
1110 A1 = 6.2832 * T1
1120 ST =  SIN (A1):CT =  COS (A1)
1130  FOR J = 1 TO J1
1140 A2 = 6.2832 * J / J1
1150 SL =  SIN (A2):CL =  COS (A2)
1160 S(J) =  - H1 * CL * ST / 2 + H2 * SL * CT / 2
1170 X1 = L * J / J1
1180 XP = X1 * SX + XS
1190 YP = YS - S(J) * SY
1200  IF J = 1 GOTO 1230
1210  HPLOT  TO XP,YP
1220  GOTO 1250
1230  HPLOT XP,YP
1250  NEXT J
1260  RETURN
2000  REM  PLOTS TRACER POSNS.
2010 A1 = T1 * 6.2832
2020 ST =  SIN (A1):CT =  COS (A1)
2030 M = 6.2832 / L
2032 ED =  EXP (M * D)
2034 SD = (ED - 1 / ED) / 2
2040  FOR J = 1 TO J2
2050 A2 = X(J) * M:SL =  SIN (A2):CL =  COS (A2)
2060 E2 =  EXP (M * (Y(J) + D))
```

```
2070 S2 = (E2 - 1 / E2) / 2:C2 = (E2 + 1 / E2) / 2
2100 DX = (H1 * SL * ST - H2 * CL * CT) * C2 / SD
2110 DY =  - (H1 * CL * ST - H2 * SL * CT) * S2 / SD
2115 DX = DX / 2:DY = DY / 2
2120 XP = (X(J) + DX) * SX + XS
2130 YP = YS - (Y(J) + DY) * SY
2140  HPLOT XP,YP
2150  NEXT J
2160  RETURN
```

WAVE2 – input and output

WAVE HT. REAL	= 2
WAVE HT. IMAG.	= −2
WATER DEPTH	= 4
WAVE LENGTH	= 24
NO. OF SURFACE PTS	= 10
SCALE FACTOR X	= 10
SCALE FACTOR Y	= 10
X OFFSET	= 10
Y OFFSET	= 100
TIME/PERIOD	= 0
ANOTHER PLOT? (Y/N)	= Y
TIME/PERIOD	= 0.25
ANOTHER PLOT? (Y/N)	= N
NO. OF TRACER PTS	= 6
X POSN.	= 6
Y POSN.	= 0
X POSN.	= 6
Y POSN.	= −2
X POSN.	= 6
Y POSN.	= −4
X POSN.	= 12
Y POSN.	= 0
X POSN.	= 12
Y POSN.	= −2
X POSN.	= 12
Y POSN.	= −4
TIME/PERIOD	= 0
ANOTHER PLOT? (Y/N)	= Y
TIME PERIOD	= 0.25
ANOTHER PLOT? (Y/N)	= Y
etc.	
TIME/PERIOD	= 0.75
ANOTHER PLOT (Y/N)	= N

Program notes

(1) Line 100 sets up arrays S, X, Y to store the surface height, and the *x, y* positions of water particles.
(2) Lines 150 to 180 input the wave heights of two standing waves which are to be combined. The water depth D and wave length L are also input.
(3) Line 200 calls subroutine 1000 to set up the screen for plotting and input scale factors, etc., for the plot. Lines 210 and 250 input the number of surface points and the time during the wave period for the surface position plot. This plot is done by calling subroutine 1100 at line 260.
(4) Lines 270 and 280 allow further plots of the surface if required. The screen is then reset for a plot of water particle positions in lines 300 to 305.
(5) Lines 310 to 340 input the number of tracer particles and their initial *x* and *y* positions.
(6) Line 350 inputs the time during the wave period at which the particle positions are plotted. The plot is made by calling subroutine 2000 at line 360.
(7) Further plots can be made for other times (expressed as time period, t/T) using lines 380 and 390. The program ends at line 400.
(8) Subroutine 1000 sets up the scale factors and additions to the *x* and *y* coordinates to fit the plots in an area of 360 × 160 units. This is done in lines 1010 to 1040. Lines 1060 to 1070 clear the screen for plotting.
(9) Subroutine 1100 plots surface positions. Lines 1140 and 1150 calculate the time-dependent parts of the standing waves.
(10) The loop from line 1130 to 1250 plots the surface over one wave length, working with J1 equally spaced points. At each point the surface height S is calculated by adding the two standing waves (lines 1140 to 1160). Lines 1170 to 1190 find the *x* and *y* positions of the surface point in the plotting units and the surface is drawn by joining these positions with a straight line from the last point. This is done in lines 1210 to 1250.
(11) Subroutine 2000 plots the position of tracer particles. Lines 2010 and 2020 find the time-dependent parts of the standing waves, lines 2030 to 2034 the denominator in the depth-dependent terms. The loop from line 2040 to 2150 then finds and plots the positions of J2 tracer particles. For each particle, lines 2050 to 2115 find the particle displacements from their initial positions. These come from the potential flow solution for the two standing waves. These positions are scaled and plotted in lines 2120 to 2140.

Example 5.3 BEM4: waves and obstacles

The first problem we shall use to test the BEM applied to waves is that of a wave in a finite depth channel which ends in a smooth vertical wall. The geometry of the problem is shown in Figure 5.9. The channel has a depth of 4 m and the wave a length L, giving $2\pi/L = 0.5$. Since L is about 12 m a length of channel equal to 12 m has been considered. We should obtain a solution in which the incident wave is completely reflected. The real and imaginary parts of the potential for the scattered wave will combine with the incident wave to leave a standing wave.

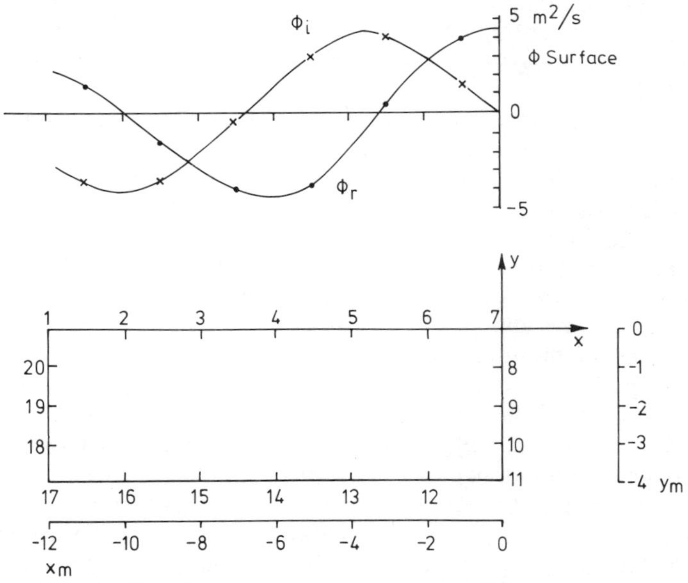

Figure 5.9 Boundary element calculation of waves meeting a vertical wall

A program to assemble the matrix equations in Section 5.5, given the boundary conditions and position of the boundary, is listed below. This is based on the program BEM2 so the definitions of X( ), Y( ), S( ), F( ), H( ), G( ) are the same, but now there are two values of S( ) for every element. In line 20, D(4), C(4), E(4) are the constants used in assembling the matrix equation. In line 21 NSF(30) is used to denote the type of boundary represented by an element. T(60,1) is the final RHS of the matrix equation as before. When the data is read, starting at line 30, we have N1, number of elements; M1, number of integration points; but now we also read

KK = $2\pi/L$, where L = wave length of incident wave, and DD = depth of water. The integration constants and element positions are read in as before in lines 32 to 40. After this, the numbers of the elements in each type of boundary 1, 2, 3, 4 are read and the boundary type stored in NSF(K) (lines 42 to 48). This is done by reading-in, in turn for each boundary type (I = 1 to 4), the number of stretches of boundary (J1) and the first and last element numbers in those stretches (K1, K2). At line 99 the size of the main matrices, N2, is calculated and the sizes set (lines 100–108). The GOSUB statement at line 110 calls a subroutine which calculates the $\partial\phi/\partial n$ caused by an incident wave of unit height. These apply at the mid-points of elements on boundary type 1. The incident wave is a progressive wave moving from left to right. At the start of this routine (lines 1000–1030) WW = ω^2/g and D(3), C(4), E(1) are calculated.

The main loop from 150 to 333 is similar to BEM2. The matrices are built up by visiting each element in turn (I = 1 to N1) to get HH = h_{ij} and GG = g_{ij}. HH and GG are used to calculate the matrix coefficients (lines 300–306) of the LHS of Equation 5.13. The RHS is calculated directly in lines 310–312. Diagonal terms (I = J) are found in lines 316–330. After this the matrix solution is straightforward (lines 560 and 570). The real and imaginary parts of the potential are then printed for each element (lines 575–620).

The wave program can be tested on a simple example, as explained above: a wave entering a tank of constant depth with a vertical end wall, shown in Figure 5.9. The wave will be completely reflected, so the solution for the scattered wave produced by the program BEM4 can be easily checked. The data for this problem are shown after the program and are input starting at line 700 of the program. There are 20 elements round the tank, four integration points on each. The wave length is $2\pi/0.5$ m and the depth of water 4 m. Coordinates of the first point in each element are given in lines 710–740 and the boundary types allocated to elements in lines 750–780. The results are plotted in Figure 5.9. The incident solution is $\phi = 4.5 \cos(kt - mx)$ and we can see that the scattered solution is

$$\phi_r = 4.3 \cos mx, \phi_i = -4.3 \sin mx$$

i.e.

$$\phi = 4.3 (\cos mx \cos kt - \sin mx \sin kt$$
$$= 4.3 \cos (kt + mx)$$

That is, a reflected wave travelling in the opposite direction to the incident wave. The amplitudes should be equal, of course. The error here (4.5 −4.3) may be due to a coarse spacing of the elements where ϕ is imposed as the boundary condition on the end wall.

A second example of wave calculations with BEM is given by the second set of data following the program. This represents the problem, sketched in Figure 5.10, of a vertical barrier in deep water. The wave length has been kept the same as for the first problem, $2\pi/L = 0.5$. The depth is input as about half a wave length to give deepwater conditions. The barrier extends to about $L/3$ so most of the wave should again be reflected. To save elements, the part of the boundary below $L/3$ in depth has been omitted, since $\partial\phi/\partial n$ and ϕ would be zero on these parts and make no contribution to the calculation. The results for ϕ on the water surface are also plotted in Figure 5.10. This time the incident wave potential has been added to the scattered wave potential calculated by the program. This shows at once that the transmitted wave is very small. The real part of the total potential ϕ_r and the imaginary part ϕ_i are both approximate $-6 \cos 2\pi/L\,(x-8)$. The total potential will thus be approximately

$$\phi = -6 \cos \frac{2\pi}{L}(x-8)(\sin \omega t + \cos \omega t)$$

$$\phi = -6 \cos \frac{2\pi}{L}(x-8)\sqrt{2} \sin\left(\omega t + \frac{\pi}{4}\right)$$

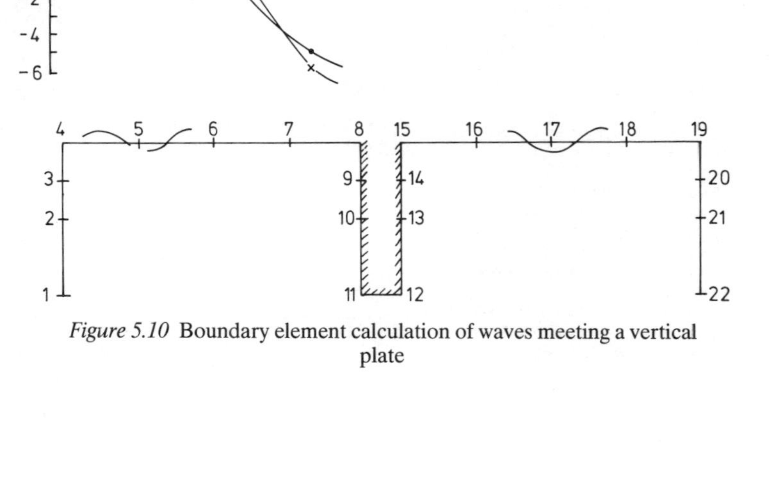

Figure 5.10 Boundary element calculation of waves meeting a vertical plate

That is, a standing wave with roughly twice the amplitude of the incident wave (2 × 4.5 = 9), which we know is the result of total reflection of the incident wave. The small difference between this pattern and the actual solution represents the small progressive wave which is transmitted under the barrier.

Program BEM4

```
10 DIM X(30,2),Y(30,2),S(60,1),F(60,1),H(60,60),G(60,60)
20 DIM D(4),C(4),E(4)
21 DIM NSF(30),T(60,1)
22 DIM FG(6),WG(6)
30 READ N1,M1,KK,DD
32 FOR I=1 TO M1
33 READ FG(I),WG(I)
34 NEXT I
35 FOR I=1 TO N1
36 READ X(I,1),Y(I,1)
38 NEXT I
40 READ X(N1,2),Y(N1,2)
42 FOR I=1 TO 4
43 READ J1
44 FOR J=1 TO J1
45 READ K1,K2
46 FOR K=K1 TO K2
47 NSF(K)=I
48 NEXT K\NEXT J\NEXT I
50 FOR I=1 TO N1-1
60 X(I,2)=X(I+1,1)
70 Y(I,2)=Y(I+1,1)
80 NEXT I
99 N2=2*N1
100 MAT H=ZER(N2,N2)
102 MAT G=ZER(N2,N2)
104 MAT S=ZER(N2,1)
106 MAT F=ZER(N2,1)
108 MAT T=ZER(N2,1)
110 GOSUB 1000
150 FOR I=1 TO N1
160 XI=(X(I,1)+X(I,2))/2
170 YI=(Y(I,1)+Y(I,2))/2
180 FOR J=1 TO N1
182 NB=NSF(J)
200 RB=SQR((X(J,2)-X(J,1))^2+(Y(J,2)-Y(J,1))^2)
202 IF J=I GOTO 316
210 SB=(Y(J,2)-Y(J,1))/RB
220 CB=(X(J,2)-X(J,1))/RB
229 HH=0\GG=0
230 FOR M=1 TO M1
232 RM=FG(M)*RB\XM=RM*CB+X(J,1)\YM=RM*SB+Y(J,1)
240 RA=SQR((XM-XI)^2+(YM-YI)^2)
250 T1=-LOG(RA)
260 SA=(YM-YI)/RA
270 CA=(XM-XI)/RA
280 T2=-(SA*CB-SB*CA)/RA
282 GG=GG+T1*WG(M)*RB
284 HH=HH+T2*WG(M)*RB
286 NEXT M
300 H(I,J)=HH+C(NB)*GG
302 H(I,J+N1)=D(NB)*GG
304 H(I+N1,J)=-D(NB)*GG
```

```
306 H(I+N1,J+N1)=HH+C(NB)*GG
310 T(I,1)=T(I,1)+GG*F(J,1)
312 T(I+N1,1)=T(I+N1,1)+GG*F(J+N1,1)
314 GOTO 332
316 GG=-RB*(LOG(RB/2)-1)
320 H(I,I)=PI+C(NB)*GG
322 H(I,I+N1)=D(NB)*GG
324 H(I+N1,I+N1)=PI+C(NB)*GG
326 H(I+N1,I)=-D(NB)*GG
328 T(I,1)=T(I,1)+GG*E(NB)*F(I,1)
330 T(I+N1,1)=T(I+N1,1)+GG*E(NB)*F(I+N1,1)
332 NEXT J
333 NEXT I
560 MAT H=INV(H)
570 MAT S=H*T
575 PRINT "ELEMENT NO.","BOUNDARY NO.","REAL POT.","IMAG. POT."
580 FOR I=1 TO N1
600 PRINT I,NSF(I),S(I,1),S(I+N1,1)
620 NEXT I
630 STOP
700 DATA 21,4,.5,6
705 DATA .0695,.174,.9305,.174,.33,.326,.67,.326
710 DATA 0,-4,0,-2,0,-1
720 DATA 0,0,2,0,4,0,6,0
730 DATA 8,0,8,-1,8,-2,8,-4
740 DATA 9,-4,9,-2,9,-1
750 DATA 9,0,11,0,13,0,15,0
760 DATA 17,0,17,-1,17,-2,17,-4
801 DATA 1,8,14
802 DATA 1,1,1
803 DATA 2,1,3,19,21
804 DATA 2,4,7,15,18
1000 REM INCIDENT VELOCITIES
1010 T1=EXP(KK*DD)\T2=EXP(-KK*DD)
1020 WW=KK*(T1-T2)/(T1+T2)
1030 D(3)=KK\C(4)=-WW\E(1)=1
1040 FOR I=1 TO N1
1050 IF NSF(I)>1 GOTO 1200
1060 XI=(X(I,1)+X(I,2))/2
1070 YI=(Y(I,1)+Y(I,2))/2
1080 RB=SQR((X(I,2)-X(I,1))^2+(Y(I,2)-Y(I,1))^2)
1090 SB=(Y(I,2)-Y(I,1))/RB
1100 CB=(X(I,2)-X(I,1))/RB
1110 SN=SIN(-KK*XI)
1120 CS=COS(-KK*XI)
1130 D1=KK*(DD+YI)
1140 D2=T1-T2
1150 Z1=(EXP(D1)+EXP(-D1))/D2
1160 Z2=(EXP(D1)-EXP(-D1))/D2
1170 OM=SQR(WW*9.81)
1180 F(I,1)=OM*(Z1*SN*SB-Z2*CS*CB)
1190 F(I+N1,1)=OM*(Z1*CS*SB-Z2*SN*CB)
1200 NEXT I
1210 RETURN
```

Data for first wave problem

	Remarks
700 DATA 20, 4, 0.5, 4	
705 DATA Standard Gauss values	
710 DATA −12, 0, −10, 0, −8, 0, −6, 0, −4, 0, −2, 0	Water surface

720 DATA 0, 0, 0, −1, 0, −2, 0, −3	RH edge
730 DATA 0, −4, −2, −4, −6, −4, −8, −4, −10, −4	Bottom
740 DATA −12, −4, −12, −3, −12, −2, −12, −1, −12, 0	LH edge
801 DATA 1, 7, 10	Boundary 1, RH edge
802 DATA 1, 11, 16	Boundary 2, Bottom
803 DATA 1, 17, 20	Boundary 2, LH edge
804 DATA 1, 1, 6	Boundary 4, top

Data for waves scattered from a vertical barrier

	Remarks
700 DATA 21, 4, 0.5, 6	
705 DATA Standard	
710 DATA 0, −4, 0, −2, 0, −1	
720 DATA 0, 0, 2, 0, 4, 0, 6, 0	Surface in front of barrier
730 DATA 8, 0, 8, 1, 8, −2, 8, −4	Barrier
740 DATA 9, −4, 9, −2, 9, −1	Barrier
750 DATA 9, 0, 11, 0, 13, 0, 15, 0	Surface behind barrier
760 DATA 17, 0, 17, −1, 17, −2, 17, −4	RH edge
801 DATA 1, 8, 14	Nodes on boundary 1
802 DATA 1, 1, 1	Nodes on boundary 2
803 DATA 2, 1, 3, 19, 21	Nodes on boundary 3
804 DATA 2, 4, 7, 15, 18	Nodes on boundary 4

Program notes

(1) Line 10 dimensions arrays for the variables used in the calculation. X and Y are the x, y coordinates of each end of the boundary element. S is the function value ϕ on the element and F the gradient $\partial\phi/\partial n$. There are two values of S and F on each element, the real and imaginary components. Real components are stored in the first half of the array and imaginary components in the second. H and G are the matrices of coefficients used in the solution.
(2) Line 20 dimension arrays D, C, E used in generating the coefficient in H and G for each of the four boundary types.
(3) Line 21 sets up arrays NSF and T which store the boundary type number and the vector on the right-hand side of the final matrix equation.

(4) Line 22 dimensions the arrays FG and WG used in the Gauss integration.
(5) Line 30 reads the data N1, M1, KK and DD. These are the number of elements, the number of Gauss points on each element,the constant $2\pi/L$, and the water depth.
(6) Lines 32 to 34 read in the constants for the Gauss integration.
(7) Lines 35 to 40 read the x and y coordinates of the first point on each element and the last point on the last element (line 40).
(8) Lines 42 to 48 read the element numbers in each type of boundary. I is the boundary type, J1 the number of strips of boundary of this type, and K1, K2 the first element and last element in a strip.
(9) Lines 50 to 80 find x and y at the second node in each element.
(10) Lines 99 to 108 set the arrays to zero and give them the correct dimensions as required by the matrix routines.
(11) Line 110 calls the subroutine 1000 to calculate $\partial\phi/\partial n$ (F) on the obstacle.
(12) The loop from lines 150 to 333 generates the coefficient in matrices H, G and T. It works round the boundary finding the contributions from each element as I increases from 1 to N1. For each value, i.e. each element there are two equations (i.e. two rows of coefficients in the matrices H, G, T), one row for the real and one for the imaginary parts.
(13) Each row contains coefficients from all the elements. These are generated in lines 180 to 332 in the loop from J = 1 to N1. Lines 182 to 229 generate the length of the element, the sine and cosine of its angle to the horizontal and set some constants for the integration over the element. In line 202 the integration is bypassed if J = I.
(14) The integration over an element is done in lines 230 to 286. This is a Gaussian integration using the constants read in at the start of the program. The value of (ϕ^*) and $(\partial\phi/\partial n)^*$ are integrated over the element to find HH and GG.
(15) Values of HH and GG are then assembled in various ways to form the coefficients in the final matrix. This follows the theory in Section 5.4 and is done in lines 300 to 312.
(16) Diagonal terms (I = J) are dealt with in lines 316 to 330.
(17) The solution to the matrix equation is achieved by standard functions in lines 560 and 570.
(18) Lines 575 to 620 print the real and imaginary parts of the velocity potential which have been calculated for each element.
(19) The data to describe a particular problem are given in lines 700 to 804. Lines 700 and 705 are data to control the running of the program. Lines 710 to 760 give x, y coordinates of element nodes and lines 801 to 804 describe the type of each stretch of boundary.

(20) Subroutine 1000 finds the values of $\partial\phi/\partial n$ at the elements on the obstacle, due to an incident wave of unit wave height. Lines 1010 to 1030 calculate w^2/g (WW) and the constants C, D and E used in finding matrix coefficients. Lines 1040 to 1200 work round the boundary, picking out the elements on the obstacle and finding $\partial\phi/\partial n$ on these elements. The real and imaginary parts of this are stored in F at lines 1180 and 1190.

Example 5.4 FDSX4: jets and weirs calculated using the (x, ψ) system

Examples of the free surface flows with large variations in surface height are shown in Figure 5.11 and 5.12. The first figure shows a jet emerging from a conduit with an angled exit lip. The position of the top streamline can be specified for the upstream half of the problem and so the starting point of the free surface does not change with the flow rate. In the second problem the whole of the upper surface of the flow is a free surface. This is the flow over a triangular section (crump) weir. Both flows are suitable for solution using the (x,ψ) coordinate system and a possible program is given below. It is called FDSX4. Line 100 stores the Y values at each point in the (x,ψ) grid. Line 120 then reads in the data: J1, number of vertical lines in grid; K1, number of streamlines in grid; N1, number of iterations; HX, x step; HS, step between grid lines; and TA, tangent of angle of streamlines at outflow boundary. Lines 120 to 130 then read in the Y values on the bottom and top streamlines and lines 140 to 180 set the starting values of Y at the internal points. This also sets the inflow boundary values and they stay fixed. This is done by linear interpolation between the top and bottom Y values. After this, data input is complete and the iteration loop is entered at line 190. The outflow values of Y are set to give the selected slope in lines 191 to 196. Then Equation 5.24 in finite difference form is solved, for each grid point in turn, in lines 200 to 320. Finally, in lines 342 to 360 the velocities and the total head are found for each grid point on the top surface (except the first and last). These are then printed. The correct free surface position is formed by adjusting the Y values at the surface until the total head is constant. This involves repeated runs of the program which could be quite lengthy on a small computer. A saving in time would be gained by modifying the program so that the repeated trials were carried out without losing the values of Y found after the previous iterations. The number of iterations for a good solution starting from unknown Y values, except on the boundary where Y is given, is usually about 50. Starting from a known solution for Y a small adjustment of the

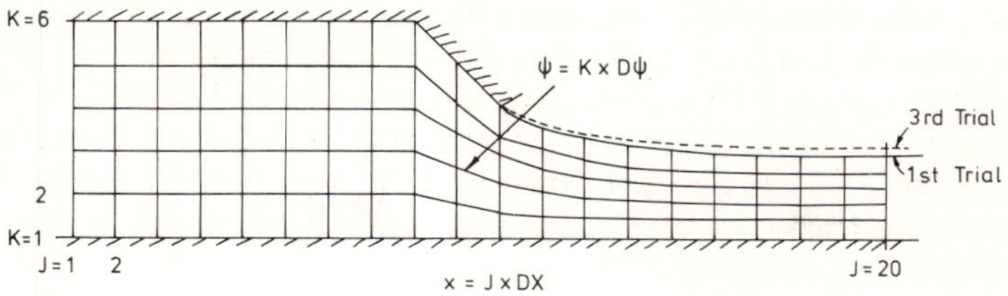

Figure 5.11 Finite difference calculation of flow from a nozzle

boundary values should need fewer iterations for a solution. The effects of over-relaxation have not been explored.

An example solved using FDSX4 can be seen in Figure 5.11. This shows a jet issuing from a conduit onto a level bed. The inflow velocity is fixed at 2.21 m/s, from which the stream function values can be found. The initial input data for the problem are given in the listing of FDSX4. The results are shown in tabular form afterwards. The initial surface position and the position after five adjustments are shown. These adjustments are made by examining the output and running the program again with new input.

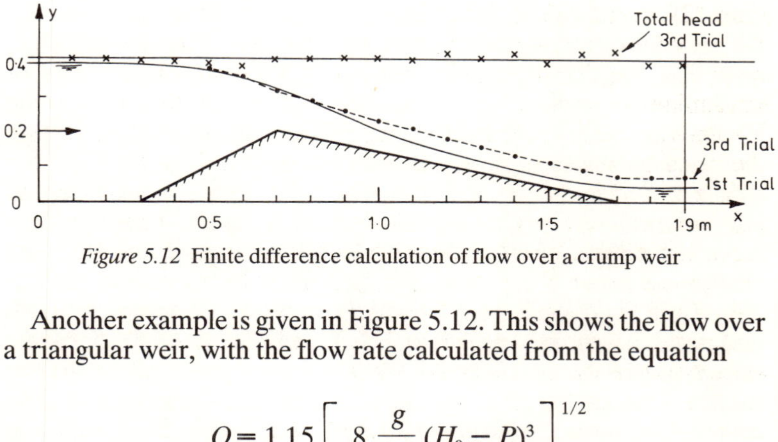

Figure 5.12 Finite difference calculation of flow over a crump weir

Another example is given in Figure 5.12. This shows the flow over a triangular weir, with the flow rate calculated from the equation

$$Q = 1.15\left[\ 8\,\frac{g}{27}\,(H_0 - P)^3\ \right]^{1/2}$$

after H_0 had been chosen as 0.4 m. The surface heights are then adjusted to get the total head as near constant as possible. These results are also shown in tabular form and in the figure. Strictly speaking, we should have assumed the flow rate Q and adjusted all the surface heights, including the upstream head, which is the quantity we really want to find in this sort of problem.

Program FDSX4

```
100 DIM Y(20,20)
110 READ J1,K1,N1,HX,HS,TA
120 FOR J=1 TO J1
130 READ Y(J,1),Y(J,K1)
140 DY=Y(J,K1)-Y(J,1)
150 FOR K=2 TO K1-1
160 Y(J,K)=Y(J,1)+DY*(K-1)/(K1-1)
170 NEXT K
180 NEXT J
190 FOR N=1 TO N1
191 FOR K=1 TO K1
192 SY=TA*(K-1)/(K1-1)
193 Y(J1,K)=Y(J1-2,K)+2*SY*HX
196 NEXT K
200 FOR J=2 TO J1-1
210 FOR K=2 TO K1-1
220 X1=Y(J+1,K)-Y(J-1,K)
230 X2=Y(J+1,K)+Y(J-1,K)
240 S1=Y(J,K+1)-Y(J,K-1)
250 S2=Y(J,K+1)+Y(J,K-1)
260 XS=Y(J+1,K+1)+Y(J-1,K-1)-Y(J+1,K-1)-Y(J-1,K+1)
270 T1=4*HX^2+X1^2
280 YT=X2*S1^2+S2*T1-XS*X1*S1/2
290 YB=2*S1^2+2*T1
300 Y(J,K)=YT/YB
310 NEXT K
320 NEXT J
330 NEXT N
342 FOR J=2 TO J1-1
344 U=(Y(J,K1)*3-Y(J,K1-1)*4+Y(J,K1-2))/(2*HS)
345 U=1/U
346 V=(Y(J+1,K1)-Y(J-1,K1))/(2*HX)
348 V=V*U
350 X1=J*HX
352 VH=(U*U+V*V)/19.62
354 TH=Y(J,K1)+VH
358 PRINT X1,Y(J,K1),VH,TH
360 NEXT J
400 DATA 20,5,50,0.5,1.381,0
410 DATA 0,2.5,0,2.5,0,2.5,0,2.5,0,2.5
420 DATA 0,2.5,0,2.5,0,2.5,0,2.5
430 DATA 0,2,0,1.5
440 DATA 0,1.3,0,1.2,0,1.1,0,1
450 DATA 0,.95,0,.95,0,.90,0,.90,0,.9
```

Results for the jet calculation – FDSX4

J	*y top streamline* (m)	*Total head on surface* (m)
1	2.5	—
2	2.5	—
3	2.5	—
4	2.5	—
5	2.5	—
6	2.5	—

7	2.5	—
8	2.5	—
9	2.5	—
10	2.0	—
11	1.5	2.47
12	1.29	2.42
13	1.18	2.41
14	1.10	2.49
15	1.05	2.57
16	1.04	2.50
17	1.03	2.50
18	1.02	2.54
19	1.02	2.51
20	1.02	2.51

Results for the weir calculation – FDSX4

J	*y top streamline* (m)	*Total head* (m)
1	0.4	0.4102
2	0.4	0.4108
3	0.4	0.4114
4	0.4	0.405
5	0.39	0.402
6	0.385	0.393
7	0.365	0.413
8	0.32	0.414
9	0.293	0.414
10	0.263	0.418
11	0.235	0.418
12	0.210	0.408
13	0.182	0.430
14	0.160	0.412
15	0.135	0.430
16	0.115	0.399
17	0.09	0.430
18	0.07	0.436
19	0.07	0.390
20	0.07	0.390

Program notes

(1) Line 100 dimensions array Y(20,20) which is the height of the streamlines in the flow.
(2) At line 110 the data read are: J1, K1, the number of columns and rows in the grid; N1, the number of iterations; HX and HS, the steps in x and stream function; and TA, the tangent of the outflow direction.
(3) Lines 120 to 180 read the streamline heights at the bottom and top of the flow. The intermediate heights are estimated by linear interpolation as a starting point for the iteration.
(4) The iteration starts at line 190. Lines 191 to 196 deal with the outflow boundary. Lines 200 to 320 apply the finite difference equation to each of the internal points. The iteration finishes at line 330.
(5) The horizontal and vertical velocities on the top streamline are calculated in lines 345 to 348. The x and y coordinates of this streamline together with the velocity head and total head are printed in lines 350 to 360.
(6) The data for each particular problem are given in lines 400 to 450.

PROBLEMS

(5.1) Write a program to calculate the velocities and accelerations at specified points within a wave. The depth of water, wave height and wave period will be specified. The wave length L must be calculated to enable the expressions for u, v, $\partial u/\partial t$ and $\partial v/\partial t$ to be found. These come from the equations

$$u = \partial\phi/\partial x,$$

$$v = \frac{\partial\phi}{\partial y}, \quad \frac{\partial u}{\partial t} = \frac{\partial}{\partial t}\left(\frac{\partial\phi}{\partial x}\right), \quad \frac{\partial v}{\partial t} = \frac{\partial}{\partial t}\left(\frac{\partial\phi}{\partial y}\right)$$

with ϕ given by Equations 5.3 and 5.6.
i.e.

$$\phi = \frac{-0.5\ Hc}{\sinh\dfrac{2\pi d}{L}} \cosh\frac{2\pi(d+y)}{L} \sin\frac{2\pi}{L}(x-ct)$$

e.g.

$$u = \frac{\pi H}{T} \frac{\cosh 2\pi\,(d+y)/L}{\sinh 2\pi \dfrac{2\pi d}{L}} \cos 2\pi \left(\frac{x}{L} - \frac{t}{T}\right)$$

$$\frac{\partial u}{\partial t} = \frac{2\pi^2}{T^2} H \frac{\cosh 2\pi\,(d+y)/L}{\sinh 2\pi \dfrac{d}{L}} \sin 2\pi \left(\frac{x}{L} - \frac{t}{T}\right)$$

Find the maximum velocity and acceleration in the wave of period 5.7 seconds in 12 m depth of water with a height of 0.45 m.

(5.2) Extend the program of Problem 5.1 to calculate the force on an element of a vertical cylinder in a wave of specified height and period. The ratio of the diameter to the wave length should be checked to see if the diffraction effect is important. The Keulegan–Carpenter number should be calculated so that the user's choice of C_M and C_D can be made easier. Find the maximum force per unit length on a pile of diameter 0.35 m in the wave of Problem 5.1, calculated for values of $C_M = 2.0$ and $C_D = 1.6$.

The total force can be found by integrating over the length of the pile, remembering that

$$\int_{-d}^{0} \cosh \frac{2\pi}{L}(d+y)\,\mathrm{d}y = \frac{\sinh 2\pi\,(d/L)}{2\pi/L}$$

The bending moment at the base of the pile comes from using

$$\int_{-D}^{0} (d+y) \cosh 2\pi(d+y)/L dy = d\,\frac{\sinh 2\pi d/L}{2\pi/L} + \left(1 - \cosh \frac{2\pi d}{L}\right) \Big/ \left(\frac{2\pi}{L}\right)^2$$

The maximum force can be found when

$$\beta = 2\pi \left(\frac{x}{L} - \frac{t}{T}\right) \text{ is given by:}$$

$$\sin \beta = \frac{2 C_M \pi D^2/4}{C_D\, DH} \frac{\sinh 2\pi\, d/L}{\cosh 2\pi(d+y)/L}$$

$$\text{or } \beta = \pi/2 \text{ for } \sin \beta > 1$$

(5.3) Write a program to calculate the reflected and transmitted wave heights from a vertical barrier. Use the approximate theory that the wave energy in a depth equal to that of the barrier is reflected. The results can be checked by comparison with Figure 5.5. Add to the program a calculation of the force on the barrier, found by integrating the pressure on the face of the barrier. This can be found from $p = \rho\, \partial\phi/\partial t$ for the case when most of the wave is reflected, and ϕ is given by the expression for a standing wave. When most of the wave is transmitted the force should be calculable in a similar way to the inertia force on a cylinder.

(5.4) Use the program BEM4 to calculate the reflected wave from a semicircular shape on the surface, as in Figure 5.5. The results should be calculated for several values of D/L so that the variation of reflection coefficient can be checked with that of Figure 5.5. The spacing of the surface element may need to be changed with the wave length so that there are always several elements in each wave length. Also find the results for a vertical barrier and compare with the approximate theory.

(5.5) Modify the program BEM4 so that pressures on the element surfaces are calculated from $\partial\phi/\partial t$ values. The forces on obstacles should then be found by integrating these pressures. Compare the force on a vertical barrier with the approximate theory of Problem 5.3.

(5.6) Change the program BEM4 so that it can calculate the waves passing over a submerged shape which is not attached to the bottom. This will require a change in the reading of node coordinates since the last node of element is now no longer the first node of the next for all elements. The direction of numbering round the boundary must also be considered. That is, if node numbers increase clockwise round the outer boundary they increase in the opposite sense round the obstacle. Check that the wave passing over a circular shape is not reflected and compare this with other shapes, for example squares.

(5.7) Use the program BEM4 to calculate the effect of waves travelling into a channel with a sloping end, compared with the vertical end of Example 5.3. The wave should still be reflected but the wave height over the sloping part of the bed will be increased.

(5.8) Use the program WAVE2 to calculate the wave envelope of a partially reflected wave formed by combining a real wave of height 1.0 m with an imaginary height of 0.5 m. Plot the paths of water particles in the same wave. Use a wave length of 24 m and a depth of 6 m.

(5.9) Calculate the surface profile of the flow over a WES type spillway operating at its design head of 1.5 m using the program FDSX4. Use the weir profile for a vertical upstream face. The upstream face will have to slope slightly from the vertical in the computer model because of the (x, ψ) coordinate system. Compare the results with Table 5.3 in Section 5.13.

(5.10) Apply the program FDSX4 to the flow from a duct of fixed size through an opening with angled sides, as in Figure 5.7. Compare the predictions of jet contraction with the analytical results (the case when the gravity term is unimportant in the free surface condition). Also calculate a case for flow from a duct onto a level bed when the gravity term is important.

(5.11) Modify the program FDSX4 so that the free surface is adjusted within the program. The final configuration should give a constant total head value on the surface. This can be tested on the flow from a duct in Problem 5.10 or the flow under a sluice gate. The simpler form of correction involving only the total head at one point to correct y at that point should be tried first. It may be useful to restrict the corrections to a particular size and form (e.g. limiting y to a smooth curve which increases or decreases).

(5.12) Calculate the effect of a gate at the top of the spillway; that is, the discharge from a sluice which has a jet on a slope instead of a flat horizontal surface.

Index